THE WOMAN WITHIN

THE
WOMAN
WITHIN

Discover the woman God made you to be

Vonette Bright

Tyndale House Publishers, Inc.
WHEATON, ILLINOIS

Visit Tyndale's exciting Web site at www.tyndale.com

The Woman Within: Discover the Woman God Made You to Be

Copyright © 2003 by Vonette Zachary Bright. All rights reserved.

First printing by Tyndale House Publishers, Inc. 2004.

Cover photo copyright © by Gildo Spadoni/Veer Inc. All rights reserved.

Designed by Catherine Bergstrom

Edited by Susan Taylor

Published in 2003 as *The Woman Within: Discover the Joy of Life in Christ* by NewLife Publications, a ministry of Campus Crusade for Christ, under ISBN 1-56399-194-2.

Library of Congress Cataloging-in-Publication Data

Bright, Vonette Z.
   The woman within : discover the woman God made you to be / Vonette Bright.
     p. cm. — (Sister circle)
   Includes bibliographical references.
   ISBN 1-4143-0052-2 (hardcover)
   1. Christian women—Religious life. I. Title.
   BV4527.B725 2004
   248.8′43—dc22   2003027373

Printed in the United States of America

10   09   08   07   06   05   04
7   6   5   4   3   2   1

I dedicate this book to the men in my life.

To my beloved husband, who mentored, loved, nurtured, protected, and challenged me. He lived every word he professed and taught me constantly by the consistency of his walk with God and the "man he was within."

To my sons, Zachary Dale and Bradley Randolph, who are now mature men, serving the Lord, with families of their own. They received the brunt of their mother's growing spiritually as they were growing physically. They learned as children to apply the principles of this book. These men continue to help me be "the woman within" that God wants me to be.

To God be the glory for what He has done in teaching these truths to me and my family and the staff of Campus Crusade for Christ.

CONTENTS

Part 4: Achieving His Purpose

Acknowledgments

More than two years ago, our dear friend William T. Greig Jr. encouraged me to upgrade a concept that our mutual friend Ethel Wilcox had written in *Power for Christian Living,* now out of print. At the same time, the suggestion was made that I revise a book I had written in 1976 titled *For Such a Time As This. The Woman Within* is the result of those conversations; however, so many things have happened in the last two years that the general concept has changed dramatically. The release of my first fiction book, *The Sister Circle,* cowritten with Nancy Moser, prompted the development of an entire line of products, and *The Woman Within* is the first of four nonfiction books in that line. Little did Bill Greig know what he was starting.

Years ago a young staff member named Carol Barrington took on the task of sitting with me for hours, forcing me to focus on any conclusions I had reached that applied to my daily life. Her availability kept me still long enough to produce the first book.

Then Brenda Josee entered my life. She is bright, beautiful, theologically oriented, and an encourager with the ability to discern my thoughts. She challenged me to once again share my life experiences that others might benefit from my more than fifty-year walk with God. Without Brenda's tenacious prodding and pushing, this book would not be a reality.

I am grateful to the New*Life* Publications staff for seeing this project through its many phases and trust the ministry impact will be a rich reward.

Thanks to my precious husband and to Dr. Luder Whitlock, internationally known theologian, who took the time to help me sort through the theology and terminology, which I hope will help to make the "Spirit-filled life" a greater reality to believers around the world who are searching for greater intimacy with God.

Foreword

$\mathcal{T}$he miraculous moment that the doctor declares, "It's a girl!" a journey begins. It is a lifelong endeavor to find the real woman hidden within the mesh of heart and emotion known as a female.

Even as toddlers we strive to find our way in the world, learning early that we can bring a man to his knees with the smallest tear. We dress dolls and begin to cultivate our maternal instincts; we skip rope and discover that strength comes easiest in numbers; we play dress-up and imitate the women we admire—all in preparation for being grown up.

We spend most of the days of our youth striving to be adults. As teenagers we paint our nails, curl our hair, and develop the fine art of flirting. As young women we learn to plot and maneuver through the jungle of eligible young men. We love to be chased yet are fearful when we are caught.

It is when we marry that we find a hint of the woman who lies within us. As newlyweds, our roles as women are further defined, and our days are filled with love. With children, jobs, and friends, the years ahead bring new roads to travel, all leading us closer to the destiny we long for. With what can be described only as a yearning to find ourselves, we begin to search with diligence, earnestly desiring to discover the woman within.

But our search for fulfillment and joy will be only as successful as the direction we take to find them. Our journey will end in frustration and loneliness unless we walk with the Companion who knows the secrets of the feminine heart.

In *The Woman Within,* Vonette Bright takes us on a journey—a journey of hope, excitement, and fulfillment. She shares how God took a frightened, fragile young woman and developed her into one of the most admired women in Christendom.

I am amazed at her insight and am honored to call her my friend. I am thankful that she has provided the directions for all of us who yearn to better understand why we were made and the purpose God has for each of us.

May God bless you as you explore the riches Vonette has discovered. She truly is a woman who knows the satisfaction of being exactly what her Creator planned her to be.

Mrs. Jack (Deb) Graham
Prestonwood Baptist Church
Dallas, Texas

A Sweet Discovery

*A*n ordinary day? Not quite! I drove the winding road leading up into the San Bernardino Mountains. The sky was blue, the clouds were white, the sun was shining—do you have a picture of the beautiful day? I pulled onto the property of Arrowhead Springs Hotel and Conference Center and found the driveway to the bungalow that was home to Dr. and Mrs. Bill Bright for thirty years. I recalled the stories Vonette had told me about the early days of planning and working to make Arrowhead Springs a place of excellence, and it certainly was.

Coming out to meet me was beautiful Vonette with the typical lilt in her step and a sweet smile on her face. What was it about her that so intrigued me? Of course, I respected her for her faithful service to God. Countless changed lives stand as testimony to her witness around the world. Our National Day of Prayer is an annual reminder to me of her tireless efforts to establish a permanent recognition of our need for God's guidance. Because of her emphasis on the ministry of hospitality, no doubt thousands of households have become more gracious. I was familiar with her life's story and admired her tremendously, yet there was something more.

She was certainly a model wife, balancing well her responsibilities as cofounder of Campus Crusade, mother to two sons, and wife to Dr. Bill Bright. When her husband would call from across the country, I had seen her face light up as she talked with tender, loving words.

I knew all this about her, but there was something else. The gracious spirit Vonette displayed was very inviting. What was that unknown element that motivated and energized her and pulled at me like a magnet? I had to know the answer.

We sat drinking tea, sharing heart-to-heart moments like teenagers—open, innocent, and transparent. What an honor for me! Then I made my discovery; I found her secret. She hadn't tried to hide it from me, I just hadn't identified it until then—that intangible quality that gave Vonette the steady, unshakable confidence to be the woman of God that she is.

Her "secret" was the fact that the Holy Spirit of God was so evident in her life. I felt an awareness of his presence in her every word. It was the woman within—influenced, nurtured, and guided by the Holy Spirit—that drew me with such intense curiosity.

The supernatural power evident in her life was not a newfound reality but something she had experienced for many years. The gentle assurance she displayed motivated me to inquire about her spiritual journey.

Vonette began to tell me how she was completely dependent on the indwelling power of the Holy Spirit to guide her thoughts, to guard her actions, and to give her strength for any situation.

For many years Vonette has had a desire in her heart to communicate the truths she has learned. *The Woman Within* is the first in a series of books designed to encourage women to discover the power and joy of a Spirit-filled life.

Scripture likens the work of the Holy Spirit to wind. We cannot see the wind; we don't know where it comes from; and we don't know where it is going. We just know it is there. Like the wind, the

Holy Spirit is sometimes turbulent, convicting, and impossible to ignore; other times it is gentle, soothing, carrying a sweet aroma.

The Holy Spirit brings an ever-present awareness of the love of Christ in our lives, and Vonette has been an expression of the Spirit of God in my life. Most authors give acknowledgment to the editor for her contribution to a project, but seldom does an editor have the privilege of expressing thanks to the author. It is a deep joy and honor to have worked with Vonette Bright and observed her example of a loving wife, mother, grandmother, and committed follower of Jesus Christ. Working with the words that express such a powerful concept as the indwelling presence of the Holy Spirit has left an indelible mark on my life. The heart and soul of Vonette Bright, reflected in the pages of *The Woman Within*, are strong and mighty in the Lord. May we all desire to exhibit in our lives the residing presence of the Holy Spirit.

Brenda Josee

Made in His Image

$\mathcal{I}$ watched curiously as the middle-aged women giggled while they waited in line to pay for their coffee. In their hands were cute little boxes of cookies, intricately designed to look like purses with handles. Covering the boxes were images of stylishly dressed ladies and brightly colored shoes. The two women captured my attention with their joyful expressions and giddy behavior. They were acting like young girls out on their own for the first time.

After my friend and I enjoyed our tea and scones—a much more sophisticated snack than cookies in a funny box—I glanced at the table where the once jubilant women were sitting. They had pulled their chairs closer together, heads almost touching, talking with obvious intensity, and one of them was handing the other a tissue to blot her eyes.

Within a few brief minutes, the sounds and sights of free-spirited friends had transformed into the hushed, serious tones of counselor and patient. The whimsical cookie boxes, now empty, had lost their appeal.

As I commented to my friend about how good it was to see two women sharing tender moments, my thought was interrupted by laughter coming from the table where there had just been tears. The two women tossed their heads back and laughed as each picked up her cookie box and clutched it to her chest.

I could only imagine what had just taken place as one woman gently counseled another and they reached a joyful conclusion. As they left the outdoor café carrying their cookie box "purses," I noticed words printed on the sides: "Sister to Sister" and "Girl-friends Forever."

This experience was a sweet confirmation of the thoughts that had been bubbling in my mind for days. How could we as Christians create a forum where women could experience the truest reality of sisterhood—where women of any age, who have faith in the God who created them, can share a little bit of life with other sisters who may think differently, dress differently, eat differently, communicate differently, and yes, even worship differently?

No woman wants to show up at an event wearing an outfit identical to another woman's, yet many women unknowingly strive for conformity to a mass-marketed image that doesn't take into consideration their individuality. Every woman, however, is a unique creation of God.

Genesis 1:27 tells us, "God created people in his own image; God patterned them after himself; male and female he created them." I think we readily acknowledge the "created" part, but somehow we lose sight of "in his own image." Maybe that is because our view of God is so blurry that it is impossible for us to see ourselves in His image.

Every woman has a life imprint stamped upon her by the hand of her Creator. Her imprint encompasses the details of her personality, temperament, abilities, style, preferences, and every other aspect of a human being. There is a unique combination for each woman, yet with all the variations every woman bears the imprint of the God of all creation—*His image.*

I believe it is the image of our Creator that allows women to relate as sisters from a very young age. Cliques, secret little neighborhood groups, summer-camp friendships, and college sororities provide environments in which women can nurture each other. We even use practical events such as baby showers, Tupperware parties, self-help groups, and so on, as opportunities to socialize.

One single element unites us, purely and simply—our sovereignly designated gender: female. As different as women may be, we are all sisters, and sisters have empathy for one another. Our hearts ache for women of the world who live in oppressive conditions.

The sisterhood of women is jarred when we hear that a woman has walked away from her husband and family, and it is jolted when we learn that a mother has killed her children. How could she? The question we ask doesn't have an answer. Only God knows the heart, but we know that every woman has an imprint on her life that God designed in her and intended to be uniquely satisfying.

For more than fifty years I have worked with women of all ages and backgrounds. My heart has been thrilled to see so many surrender their lives to Christ and discover the potential of the woman within them. But I continue to desire to reach women with the exciting news that the God who created them loves them and can transform them from the inside out.

The woman within is the real you, the you that God created in His image, with a unique role to fulfill in His master plan. When God's love fills the heart of a woman, there are no limits to what she can accomplish.

Understanding why we think and act the way we do is very liberating. Going through life unaware that God has given us special abilities and a unique purpose is a sad prospect and can make for a wearisome life.

This book, *The Woman Within*, was written with one goal. My heart's desire is to see women of faith connecting, loving, caring, serving, and supporting each other with such genuine love that women who do not know Christ will be drawn to those who do and will want to meet Him.

Please read this book with the eyes of your heart open and your spirit expectant. God is so faithful, and only He can satisfy the woman within you!

Vonette Bright

PART 1

ADMITTING OUR NEED

I take joy in doing your will, my God,
for your law is written on my heart.

PSALM 40:8

If you wish to live richly, deeply
and spiritually, you must cultivate
the "world within." It is a thrilling
world . . . with the Heavenly
Father as our companion.

THE NASHVILLE TENNESSEAN

ONE

Having It All

*W*hat were the dreams you had for your future? Are you realizing them?

When I was much younger, I liked to imagine my life as a well-directed movie being filmed for the big screen. I was sure that my life story would depict the wholesome American dream with the cast of characters carefully scripted to create the plot that would fulfill my desires. I had a long list of things I wanted to do and experience. For a time in my twenties, it seemed like things were going to work out as I wanted.

But, of course, that's not the way things played out. As you probably know, life is not neatly packaged. Our dreams often turn out to be just that—dreams. In fact, at times it feels as if living is more like a movie where the projector has malfunctioned, making the scenes fly by in a panic and the conversations sound like a maniacal Donald Duck. And I can't find the switch that slows everything down.

You probably have stories from your own life that fit what I'm describing. If you're a working woman, you most likely have some point of stress at your job that keeps you off balance. Certainly, if you're the mother of preschoolers, you know the experience of seeing chaos spread faster than you can run behind to create order. And my heart goes out to you if you are in the turmoil of parenting teenagers.

One of the dreams I had in childhood was to live in a beautiful house with my husband and children. In my thirties I realized that dream! My husband, Bill, and I were living in a gorgeous home that resembled a Moorish castle in the exclusive area of Bel Air, California. We were just minutes from the UCLA campus and were involved in the lives of hundreds of young men and women who would be tomorrow's leaders. For a girl from the little town of Coweta, Oklahoma, this was a greater realization than I had envisioned for my life.

For a girl from the little town of Coweta, Oklahoma, this was a greater realization than I had envisioned for my life.

But if you had peeked behind the closed doors of my castle, you would have found that I thought life was more ideal for Bill than for me. I felt overwhelmed with all my responsibilities. I was a new mother of our son, Zachary Dale, trying to adjust to a very different pattern of living dictated by this tiny being who had such a tight grip on my heartstrings. At the same time, our ministry to students was growing like a fresh seed planted in fertile soil. That meant that we had students coming in and out of our house at all hours. At first, I took on the extra housework as a challenge. Because I had graduated from college as a home economist, I believed I had the necessary skills to manage the job. With the fervor of my youth, I was absolutely confident that I could keep a twenty-room house running smoothly, see to all of little

4

Zachary's needs and wants, plus find time to maintain a full schedule of meetings with female coeds.

I'm sure you can guess what happened. The whole spectacle turned into that out-of-control film, and I soon felt depressed, discouraged, and even put upon. Many times while 250 students and friends laughed and visited in the other rooms, I stood at the kitchen sink staring at stacks of dirty dishes and lamented, *Why isn't someone in here helping me?*

Don't get the wrong idea; this scenario was not a case where my husband was insensitive and expected his wife to do the behind-the-scenes work while he got the glory. I was privileged to have married a kind and humble man who considered me a treasure that God had given him. Even back then, my heart was beside his in the ministry we were sharing. Yet there were many times when events worked out to what I thought was my disadvantage. Because of my bad attitude, I didn't put much weight on all of Bill's responsibilities and problems, but my own I could describe in minute detail. At those times I found that I couldn't control my feelings of resentment and martyrdom. Even more troubling, I wasn't sure how I could change my attitude. Sadly, I had achieved my dreams, but now I felt unhappy.

How things changed is central to the story I want to tell you, but first, let's explore the problem by considering what women face today.

The Twentieth-Century Woman

During my adult life I've seen many transformations in our society. One of the most significant is how the role of women has changed. When I first attended Texas Women's University, most women had limited career options such as nursing and teaching. Since then, the women's movement has helped change people's thinking.

I'm all for women being able to use their talents and follow their desires to the fullest extent, but we have let the feminist agenda and other social pressures pile on stress and problems that our predecessors rarely experienced. We have been told that we can "have it all"—a career, family, and plenty of leisure time. Many women are discovering how unfulfilling it is to live an overcommitted, hectic life.

Do you remember a singer by the name of Karen Carpenter? She was a young, attractive woman who had a voice so pure that many people considered it the most expressive in popular music. She and her brother, Richard, reached the top of the music charts in the 1970s and early 1980s and were a best-selling group. Career, success, fame, fortune, a fan club—Karen seemed to have it all.

It wasn't long, however, before the media uncovered a problem in her life: she suffered from anorexia nervosa. She deteriorated from a vibrant, healthy young woman to a walking skeleton. Her loved ones were panic-stricken and tried to help her in any way they could.

Karen finally recognized the harm she was doing to herself and started on the road to recovery, but her efforts were too late. On February 4, 1983, her weakened heart gave out; she was only thirty-two years old.

I have spent the last five decades working with women across the spectrum of life and observing how they handle life's issues.

One thing I've noticed: not one of them "has it all." Some prominent women have acknowledged the impossibility of this goal. Recently, Karen Hughes, advisor to President George W. Bush, resigned her position at the White House to move back to Texas and spend more time with her family. She is an example of a person who had to make a hard choice, but I believe the more rewarding choice.

The Dilemma for the Woman Within

You may be in a place right now where you know how hollow the promise is that you can "have it all." Most of us, at some point, will encounter daunting problems in life. Can you find your situation in any of these?

- Going through the pain of divorce
- Grappling with a life of singleness
- Engulfed in the death of a loved one
- Wrestling with a rebellious teenager
- Stuck in a demanding, unfulfilling job
- Struggling with a debilitating illness
- Haunted by a poor self-image
- Wallowing in depression
- Depressed by mountains of household chores
- Fearing disaster around every corner
- Living in an empty nest
- Drowning in loneliness
- Devastated by widowhood

Even reading this list can make a person feel discouraged. I'm sure you could add a few items from your experiences.

Have you ever felt that your "woman within," the tender place inside your heart that feels the pain and the joy, is crying out but no one can hear? Do you feel as if your inner self is being suffocated by the circumstances of life or the demands of others?

In my parents' day, women often lost themselves in their husbands and children and may have neglected their own needs because they were too busy serving others. They ignored their own personal growth, and consequently many felt depressed, lonely, and unfulfilled.

Have things changed that much? It's true that women now have so many more opportunities and can develop their talents and abilities and achieve success in their own right. But having a career, financial success, the ability to follow your dreams, and the life of a "super mom" do not satisfy the inner longings of the soul. Have we just replaced one set of oppressive obligations with another?

Before you think I'm describing a life of hopelessness, let me tell you that there is a different way to exist. I have lived with incredible stress for most of my life, but I have enjoyed the journey with total abandon. Many of the women I admire most are fully satisfied with their lives and experience a deep joy in daily living. But their success is not due to balancing a career, family, and everything else. Instead, successful women have faced tremendous sorrows and mountainous problems and have been victorious in spite of it all. That's because they have relied on God for the solution to their problems.

I have experienced this truth in my own life and have seen it transform women struggling with despair into excited, optimistic, life-loving women. It all comes down to finding the spiritual purpose and plan for your life.

What's the Plan?

In this book I want to encourage you to follow a new way of living—according to God's plan. He created us as we are, with intricate feelings, desires, and hopes. He understands the pressures we face and the society in which we live. And most wonderful of all, He is vitally interested in every hurt we experience, every dream we abandon, every temptation we struggle with. Because He formed each of us as a unique creation, He has an intimate knowledge of every desire in our hearts and thought in our minds. And He loves us more deeply than we can ever imagine.

As we seek together to learn what God says in His Word and what He is waiting to do for us, we will discover the perfect plan He has created for you and me. Our journey of joy in knowing God will require four steps of faith:

1. Admit your need to God.
2. Accept His unlimited grace.
3. Acquire skills to live a full life.
4. Achieve your ultimate purpose in life.

No worthwhile journey is ever taken without a willingness to endure to the end. As we search the mind of God revealed in the Scriptures, be prepared for challenges and insights that will change the way you think and live. I urge you to make a commitment right now to place your life in God's hands and open your-self to what He has in store for you. Don't be afraid; He is the gentle shepherd of the Bible and will always handle our inner desires and hurts with the greatest tenderness. But also be prepared to grapple with areas of rebellion or indifference to God's will that you may uncover.

Begin Your Journey

I'm excited about your journey to discover the woman within. Over the years I've found God to be faithful and merciful. He has given each of us the privilege of knowing Him as an intimate friend—something for which I am so grateful! And I know you will be too.

As you read this book, I encourage you to find one or more friends with whom you can share your journey. As women, we have a tremendous capacity to form rela-tionships that build us up and help us to be accountable to what we know we should do. I like to call these friendship ties "Sister Circles." You will enjoy reading and apply-ing the principles in this book so much more if you share your adventures in spiri-tual growth with other women.

As you read this book, I encourage you to find one or more friends with whom you can share your journey.

However, if you find it impossible to create a Sister Circle, begin a diary in which you can record the discoveries God leads you to and the areas for improvement that He brings to mind. In this diary write out your prayers, list your praises, or just describe your sorrows and joys. Turn to the list of resources in the back of this book to find other materials to help you on your journey.

Before you begin the next chapter, take a moment to thank God for how wonderfully He created you and for how much He loves you. After all, in Christ we truly do "have it all," for we are complete in Him (Colossians 2:10).

TWO

Giving It All

 $\mathcal{W}$ hen you shop in a mall, how do you determine where to go?

Most large shopping centers have strategically positioned directories to help shoppers find a store and chart a course to get there. To locate their destination, some people choose a random approach of scanning the floor plan, although it may take a while to find the store they need. Other people look for the store name listed alphabetically under the desired category. Once they locate the store on the map, shoppers must identify where they are in relation to the store and plan their route.

Occasionally I feel so certain I know where the store is that I ignore the directory, navigating the mall with my memory as my guide. Since I don't shop frequently enough to stay familiar with store locations, I can waste valuable time by depending on my own abilities.

The scenario I have just described is a good picture of the spiritual condition of many people. They realize that God exists, but they don't plan how to relate to Him; they just toss up a prayer now and then or follow a pathway of their own choosing. Neither of these is an effective way of knowing God. In fact, "going it on our own" will lead us further away from God. And not knowing the direct route will get us off the right path.

Have you ever noticed what the world believes about God? I'm sure you've listened to what television programs have to say about him. Most of the time, the message is pretty shallow—and even critical toward religion. The secular world has little idea of what they miss by not knowing the God of the universe, who not only positioned the stars in space but is also interested in the details of their lives.

Where It All Began

I can remember when I first heard that if I were the only person in the universe, Christ would still have died for me, and that I could know and experience His love and plan for my life. I immediately thought: *If God has a plan for my life, I certainly wish He would hurry up and show me what it is.* I had just finished college, was in the midst of a relationship with a wonderful man, and held a teaching contract in my hand. At the same time, I was trying to figure out why I was put on this earth, and all I got for my quest was confusion.

You know what my problem was? I had to admit that I had a need. I had tried going to church and living a moral life, desperately attempting to do what was right, but still felt an inner vacancy. I thought that all I had to do was try a little harder to be good, and God would approve. This view, however, was not filling the emptiness I felt inside. It seemed the more I gave out, the less I got in return.

I wasn't struggling with life because of some horrible event in my past or some tragedy that I couldn't face. My life had not been a fairy tale, but I did know the blessing of a happy childhood. As the oldest of four children, my earliest memories include the activities of a wholesome life.

When I was a young girl, I determined to set my standards high, and my church background and home training prepared me to stay morally pure for the man I would marry. But in college my confidence in Christianity wavered, and I began to question the reality of my faith. My prayers seemed shallow and ineffective. In high school my major interest centered on church-related activities, but in those early days of college, Bible reading was meaningless. Doubts came, and I was not faithful in church attendance.

But my life was about to change radically. On a lovely summer day after my freshman year in college, I received a letter from Bill Bright. I remembered him from our school days and was impressed by a speech I had heard him deliver when I was in the seventh grade. Bill was in business in California, and his stationery read "Bright's California Confections." I read the letter several times before sharing it with my father. When Dad read it, he said, "Well, our hometown boy has gone away and made good. Now he's going to come home for his bride."

I decided that I would not allow William R. Bright to think I was thrilled to hear from him, so I ignored the letter. Months later and settled back into college life, I was cleaning out a desk drawer and came across the letter. I told my roommate some of my thoughts about this unusual young man from my hometown. She encouraged me to write to him. It had been almost three years since I had seen Bill Bright, but I spent an evening writing a ten-page letter.

That was the beginning of a beautiful romance in which the correspondence flourished as we began to write daily. I received flowers, candy, a telegram, or telephone call every week. My long-distance courtship became the talk of the campus. I was truly swept off my feet.

When Bill came to visit me, we had a delightful time together. After talking about what had happened in the years since we had seen each other, Bill proposed marriage, and I accepted.

As we continued our relationship over the next three years, many spiritual questions plagued me. Bill had a deep religious faith. He sent me passages of Scripture to read, but they just did not have the same meaning to me as they did to him. He would also ask me to pray about concerns. I began to realize I was engaged to a man to whom Christ meant a great deal, and yet Christ was not real to me.

I began to realize I was engaged to a man to whom Christ meant a great deal, and yet Christ was not real to me.

I decided Bill had become a religious fanatic and that somehow he must be rescued from this fanaticism. At the same time, Bill was beginning to think that perhaps I was not a Christian. He knew he could not marry me until there was a change in my spiritual life.

Then Bill invited me to come to California for a college briefing conference. My parents were opposed to my going even though our engagement had been announced and the marriage was planned for September. As I walked across the stage to receive my degree, someone handed me a telegram from Bill, congratulating me on my graduation. As I returned to my seat, I knew that I had to go to California. If there was a chance to save our relationship, I needed to try. My motive was to save Bill from the influence of those I considered fanatics. Unknown to me, Bill's motive was for me to find Christ.

A Big Change

When I arrived in Los Angeles, Bill and I went to a college conference at Forest Home, a Christian conference center in California. There I met young people who possessed a quality of life I had never seen. They vibrantly shared their faith. Their statements annoyed me because I felt that Christianity was something personal that you didn't freely discuss. I tried to put their comments out of my mind, yet I admired them and liked their quality of life. So I listened to statements like "Let me tell you about my answer to prayer" or "Just look what I read in the Bible today!" I asked them how they knew God had answered their prayers or how they knew what the Bible really says. I wanted to find out how they knew God so personally.

One evening as Bill and I were discussing the difference in these young people, I realized that his faith was right for him; but I had tried religion, and it just wouldn't work for me. I knew I did not want to stand in the way of his relationship with God, so I concluded that perhaps the best thing to do was simply bow out of his life. At the end of the week, I would return his ring, and we would go our separate ways.

Then Bill asked me to talk with Dr. Henrietta Mears, who was the inspiration of the six-thousand-member Sunday school at the First Presbyterian Church of Hollywood. She later founded Gospel Light Publications to provide Sunday school lessons, and because of her vision, the Forest Home conference grounds, where Bill and I attended our first college briefing, became a great spiritual oasis for thousands of vacationers.

Miss Mears was expecting me when we met, and what I did not know was that the entire staff was praying for me. Miss Mears explained that she had taught chemistry in Minneapolis and that she could understand how I was thinking. I had minored in chemistry in college, so everything had to be practical and logical to me.

As she explained from the Bible how I could be sure I knew God, she used familiar terminology. She said that God loved me, and if I had been the only person in the entire world, He would have done everything He could to reveal himself to me. He had a plan and purpose for me that was far beyond anything I could possibly imagine. However, before I could know that plan and purpose, it was necessary for me to know God.

She explained that just as a person going into a chemistry laboratory to perform an experiment follows the periodic table of elements, so it is possible for a person to enter God's laboratory and follow His formula for knowing Him. The reason man does not know God is that he is sinful and separated from God. When she said, "Man is sinful," my reaction was, *Speak for yourself. That doesn't apply to me. I've worked at this business of being a good girl.* Then she showed me Romans 3:23: "All have sinned; all fall short of God's glorious standard." She explained that sin is falling short of God's perfect standard for us and breaking His rules for living. I had to admit that I fell short of this standard—and even my own standard—many times. I was a person who kept lists of areas of my life to improve, and I worked desperately at being more loving, considerate, helpful, and neat.

Miss Mears went on to show me Romans 6:23: "The wages [result] of sin [falling short of God's standard] is death [spiritual separation from God], but the free gift of God is eternal life through Christ Jesus our Lord." I finally began to consider who Jesus Christ is, and I had to admit that I did not really know Him.

Then Miss Mears showed me John 14:6 where Jesus says, "I am the way, the truth, and the life. No one can come to the Father except through me." I realized I had tried to live a good life, had kept a high moral standard, and had been active in church, but despite this, there was something missing in my life. None of these things could provide a personal relationship with God. For the first time in my search for truth, I admitted that perhaps Jesus Christ was the "ingredient" I was missing. I turned to Miss Mears and asked, "If Jesus Christ is the way, then how can I know Him?"

Miss Mears responded, "In Revelation 3:20 Christ says, 'Look! Here I stand at the door [entrance to your heart and life] and knock. If you hear me calling and open the door, I will come in, and we will share a meal as friends.' Receiving Christ is a matter of turning your life completely over to Him—your will, your emotions, your intellect. It is as if we walk out of our lives and Jesus Christ walks in. He takes control."

If what she told me was true, I had absolutely nothing to lose and everything to gain. I bowed my head to pray and asked Jesus to come into my heart and take control. At that moment God became a reality in my life.

At the time I received Christ, the picture that came to my mind was one I shall never forget. I was standing in utter darkness on the edge of a diving board. (I do not swim; as a matter of fact, I almost lost my life in a swimming course in college. I passed the course but have not jumped off a diving board since.) In the dream I did not know whether or not I could swim, but I knew I had to jump—and I found out that I could swim and that God is real! I gave Him all my trust, and He didn't fail me.

From that day on, God's direction in my life became a reality as I found my strong will and temper easier to control. The Bible became a living Book and a guide for my life. I could not have imagined how the decision I had made would impact the rest of my life, but it has and is continuing to be the greatest influence.

From that day on, God's direction in my life became a reality as I found my strong will and temper easier to control.

On December 30, 1948, Bill and I were married, and the greatest adventure of my life began, not just in my new role as wife, but also in my new life as a believer.

Back to Basics

The secret for fulfillment in life, then, is to admit that we can't do anything on our own to accomplish it. This is because, as Miss Mears so clearly explained to me through Bible verses, as humans we are bound up in sin. Sin limits our lives and keeps us from knowing God. Only He has the solution for releasing us from our sin so we can experience peace, love, joy, and contentment.

The Bible tells us that right now we are in one of two positions: a child of God or child of the devil (John 1:12-13; 8:44). Where you are will make an eternal difference. Have you ever come to the point where you have examined your life and admitted to God that you are a sinner in need of His forgiveness? Have you ever told Him that you know He loves you and that you want to have a relationship with Him?

Admitting your need for God's forgiveness in Jesus Christ is the most important decision you will ever make. When you do, these are just a few of the events that will happen:

- You will go from a future of eternal punishment to eternal life (1 John 5:11-12).
- Every sin you have ever committed will be forgiven by God because of His Son's death on the cross (Acts 10:43).
- You will receive the Holy Spirit, who lives in every child of God (Romans 8:9, 14).
- You are entitled to an inheritance from your heavenly Father (1 Peter 1:3-4).
- You are able to accomplish the plan that God has for you (Ephesians 2:10).
- You will find true fulfillment (John 10:10).

If you have never made the decision to become part of God's worldwide family, or if you are not sure you have done so, turn to the back of the book. "Beginning Your Journey of Joy" will explain how you can know God intimately. I have learned that it makes no difference *when* you received Christ, but it is extremely important that you know that you have received Him—that Christ right now is in your life and that if you died today, you would spend eternity with Christ in heaven. You cannot mature (grow) spiritually until you have assurance that Christ is in your life. Take a few moments right now to ensure your future with God. Give Him your heart and your life.

The Bible calls this decision "the new birth." (Read about this in John 3:1-21.) Being born again is such an apt description for what happens. God gives you new life, one that will last forever. Your heart is made fresh and clean, free of its sin-guilt. It's like waking up after a smog-filled night to the fresh, crisp smell of a spring rain. Although women have many different emotional experiences when they are born spiritually (from exuberant joy to quiet peace), feelings are not important. If you sincerely turned your life over to Jesus as your Savior and Lord, you can be sure that God has forgiven your sins and made you a part of His family. We can rejoice together that you have a bright new future!

Continuing the Journey

Once you are sure you have a relationship with God, you begin a lifelong journey that will amaze you. When I received Jesus Christ as my Savior back in that conversation with Henrietta Mears, I had no idea what God would do with my future. It was so much more than I expected! My walk with God hasn't been simple or easy, but if we are honest, we will admit that a life with no challenges would be boring. On the other hand, facing challenges that defeat us is a tragedy. I am so grateful to God that He not only chose my pathway through life but that His Holy Spirit enables me to live above my circumstances and to experience His power to change me. As you read along in this book, I will share some of the trying and thrilling times in my journey with God.

Bill believed the Scriptures from the time He received Christ. I declare He was "born running" and never lost that original zeal. I, on the other hand, have sometimes struggled to see these truths lived out in my life. I could not proclaim something to others that was not true for me in daily living. I struggled with ambition, impatience, anger, dominant personality, desire to control, possessiveness—you name it. I needed a transformation! Bill was patient, loving, understanding, and ministering to me through words and actions. I learned so much from his deep faith.

Another individual who taught me much about the Christian life was Ethel Wilcox, who this generation does not know. She was a lovely, godly woman whose life and ministry touched the lives of thousands of people, including my own. She was so spiritual, and so practical in her application of Scripture, that her illustrations became "hooks" on which I could hang spiritual truths. Those scriptural principles have continued to be applied daily and made transferable through the years.

In her emphasis on victorious living, Ethel Wilcox helped me to connect the supernatural to the practical in a way that has allowed me to live a more consistent and spiritually productive life. There is no other way to make faith real, consistent, and transferable than to submit totally to the Holy Spirit and to invite Him to live the life of Jesus in and through you.

If you have been a Christian for some time and do not feel victorious or happy and your spirit seems beaten down, you, too, will find God's solution. He not only offers us eternal life, He also walks with us moment by moment while we live on this earth. He enables us to conquer the monsters of adversities. He also gently heals our inner hurts and builds up our inadequacies. The rest of this book will show you how you can experience the most from life through God's indwelling presence.

If the person and ministry of the Holy Spirit is not real in your life, I trust this book will help you experience that reality. If you do know the reality of the Holy Spirit in your life, I trust this book will confirm the joy and victory you know every day and will help you in some way to share the truth of the Spirit-filled life with others. To live anything less is, as my husband said, "living in self-imposed spiritual poverty."

A Woman's Role

I have worked with women for many decades, and I am convinced that we have a much greater influence than we give ourselves credit for. We also have so many possibilities ahead of us. What seems like an overwhelming task when we are trying to "have it all" turns into a glorious victory when we "give it all" to God.

Let's take this journey step-by-step so that we can be sure to address the heart issues of our inner woman that are so prevalent in our lives. Just as a bad cut doesn't heal in a day, so we must take time to heal our souls. God is the Great Physician who can accomplish the task.

We'll begin in the next section by exploring the grace of God toward His frail human creation. Once you understand who He is and the depth of His love and care for you, you will trust Him fully to help you become the woman He made you to be.

PART 2

ACCEPTING
HIS GRACE

Since we have been made right in God's sight by faith, we have peace with God because of what Jesus Christ our Lord has done for us. Because of our faith, Christ has brought us into this place of highest privilege where we now stand, and we confidently and joyfully look forward to sharing God's glory.

ROMANS 5:1-2

Whether a man arrives or does not arrive at his own destiny—the place that is peculiarly his—depends on whether or not he finds the Kingdom within and hears the call to wholeness—or holiness, as another might say. The man who hears that call is chosen. He does not have to scramble for a place in the scheme of things. He knows that there is a place which is his and that he can live close to the One who will show it to him. Life becomes his vocation.

ELIZABETH O'CONNOR,
JOURNEY INWARD, JOURNEY OUTWARD

THREE

Unmerited Favor

$\mathscr{I}$ remember so clearly the first time I held my new baby in my arms. There I was, cradling a bundle of blue blankets wrapped around a precious gift from God. I had held many newborns before, but this bundle was different—the baby boy I cradled in my arms was mine. He was mine to feed, protect, and raise in "the admonition of the Lord." I had heard that phrase so many times as pastors delivered sermons on parenting. What did it really mean, and could I do it?

Every mother will understand when I say that in one moment my emotions went from indescribable joy to overwhelming anxiousness. While I felt confident that my husband would be a good father, I wasn't so certain about my own skills. Was I up to this daunting task of motherhood?

Today Zachary Bright is a grown man, and when I observe him interacting with his wife and children or hear him deliver a sermon, my heart is filled with gratitude for God's grace that allowed me the privilege of being his mother. Those anxious moments I experienced as a new mother are dim memories that pale in the glow of my love for the man my son has become.

I wish Tyndale's *New Living Translation* had been around years earlier; it clarifies Scripture so beautifully. Ephesians 6:4 instructs us to bring up our children "with the discipline and instruction approved by the Lord."

Those anxious moments I experienced as a new mother are dim memories that pale in the glow of my love for the man my son has become.

Our second child, Bradley, benefited from my experience with Zac. I don't remember feeling quite so anxious when Bradley was born. Brad recently completed writing a book, and as I read and reread the manuscript, my heart overflowed again with gratitude for God's grace in Brad's life and for his insight that could impact our culture for righteousness. Maybe this insight is the evidence of being raised in the "admonition of the Lord."

Motherhood is a permanent state of being. The duties and responsibilities change with time, but a mother's heart is always open to her children. Becoming a mother changes a woman's life completely, and I can't help but relate this transformation to the experience of being born into the family of God. Accepting Christ brings you into God's family, and your life is forever changed.

Do you remember the first time someone called you "mother"? Didn't it sound strange, yet thrilling? Your new role altered the way you thought of yourself. Many things you did in the past, such as going to the mall alone, didn't seem as important anymore. It was now more fun to take the baby wherever you went.

When you became a new believer, your life changed even

more completely. You looked at yourself differently—as a child of the living God. Many of your previous interests lost their shine as you began to develop a relationship with God and learned to enjoy what He enjoys.

But new disturbing thoughts may have popped up. What does God expect of His child? Should I do this or avoid doing that? What happens if I blow it?

Parenting is not easy. Each time you feel you have conquered a stage, your son or daughter grows into new challenges. How simple a toddler's temper tantrums seem when your teenager is bending the curfew rules! How easy handling play dates seems when you are worrying about your teen coming home from a real date. But, oh, the joy of seeing that baby learn to feed himself, take his first step, begin his first day of school, go out on his first date, and graduate from high school! I must admit I was thoroughly unprepared for each new challenge of motherhood, but I also had the privilege of reveling in Zac's and Brad's accomplishments.

Our changing role as parents is similar to our identity as children of God. As Christians, we will always face new challenges as we mature spiritually and learn to become more like Jesus Christ. Sometimes we will despair because we fail God so bitterly. Other times we will rejoice because of the marvelous work God has accomplished by the Holy Spirit in and through us, thereby glorifying Him. Trying or striving to live the Christian life is too much. Christ wants to live His life in and through us.

If you have been a believer for some time and feel discouraged, let me encourage you. As a parent, you encounter problems—yes, even deep hurts—that you never expected. Sometimes the problems come from your own inadequacies as a parent; other times, from the disobedience of your child. Yet you don't give up. Think of your spiritual role the same way. Motherhood is a role you chose—and you don't throw in the towel when times get tough. Becoming a part of God's universal family is also a role you chose—but now you no longer live in your own strength.

The joy of walking with God is far greater than that of being a mother. And this joy lasts forever. But as with anything worthwhile, tough times will come. Keep going. I can assure you that God has a solution for those experiences too.

Knowing God Is Key

The question then becomes: How do we live in God's family in a way that helps us progress in our spiritual growth and keeps us from falling back into our old ways? The key is in trusting God completely. Knowing who God is helps us to trust Him.

As women, many of us struggle with issues of low self-esteem. Perhaps this stems from the sensitive nature of women, or maybe we have more trouble dealing with life's harshness, but as a gender we do devalue ourselves more than men do. This feeling of having little worth interferes with our maturation process in all areas of life—including the spiritual area.

That is why it is so important to understand God's love and grace. When we place our hearts in God's hands and trust Him with our lives, He reveals himself adequate in allowing us to withstand attacks from temptation in the world, from the evil one (Satan), and from our own fleshly desires.

God is your creator and your lover. Since He made every

single atom in your body and knows every single thought in your mind—good and bad—he is not surprised by what you do or what you think. His love is unconditional, based on His grace, not on what you do to merit His love.

God builds us up so we can withstand attacks from temptation in the world, from Satan, and from our own fleshly desires.

Our world teaches us that people will love us if we have money, are talented, treat them wonderfully, and smell good. But if we don't have the qualities that they want in a friend, forget it. We may still get handouts, like the homeless, but no one will truly love us in spite of who we are. That's what's so amazing about God! He knows the deepest recesses of your heart, the places that you never reveal to others because you are afraid of rejection. Yet He loves you with an eternal love that nothing can take away.

The apostle Paul writes about God's love in the book of Romans. Read the following verses, mull over them, let them sink into your soul. Perhaps they are so familiar to you that you skip over the meaning each time you hear them. This time listen closely to what God is telling you about how much you mean to Him: "I am convinced that nothing can ever separate us from his love. Death can't, and life can't. The angels can't, and the demons can't. Our fears for today, our worries about tomorrow, and even the powers of hell can't keep God's love away. Whether we are high above the sky or in the deepest ocean, nothing in all creation will ever be able to separate us from the love of God that is revealed in Christ Jesus our Lord" (Romans 8:38-39).

Insert the reason that you feel unworthy into this verse:

"Nothing can ever separate us from His love. Being overweight can't, and being poor can't. Being slow to learn, quick to anger, and even having no education can't keep God's love away."

Next, put assurance in the passage in Romans next to this one in Psalm 139: "You made all the delicate, inner parts of my body and knit me together in my mother's womb. Thank you for making me so wonderfully complex! Your workmanship is marvelous—and how well I know it. You watched me as I was being formed in utter seclusion, as I was woven together in the dark of the womb. You saw me before I was born. Every day of my life was recorded in your book. Every moment was laid out before a single day had passed" (vv. 13-16).

These verses give us so much comfort. When we know how well God knows us, how marvelously He formed us, and how carefully He looks to our future, we can rest in His love. He doesn't see our limitations; He sees our potential. He created us with the qualities that will fit into His plan for our lives. We don't need to be perfect, well educated, rich, or live in a gorgeous house. He just wants us as we are and will produce in each one of us an original "you."

What does He want in return for His love? Our love. That's all. He wants us to serve Him out of a heart of gratitude and love, not out of duty. We see the beauty of this transaction in our children's lives. When we give a child a chore, it delights our hearts when He obeys with a desire to please us. When we give this same child a chore and he does the work grudgingly or out of fear of what will happen if he doesn't do it, we don't feel the same satisfaction. That is exactly how we should relate to God, out of a love response because He loved us first. This is what grace is all about.

The Joy of Grace

Let me give you some facts about God's grace. When you under-stand His grace, you will know His heart for you.

A popular definition for God's grace is "unmerited favor." But that is only the beginning point. These facts about God's grace will assure you even more of His unlimited love for you:

- Through grace, God reveals His nature and the glory of His Son's sacrifice for us.
- Grace is a gift. We never have to repay God for what He gives us.
- Through grace, we receive all the infinite resources of God, including salvation, a new life, and eternity in heaven with Him.
- God will never withhold His grace because of something we do that displeases Him.

We must base our self-worth on the fact that God loves us so much. If the God of the universe, who is continually praised by the angels and could relate to anyone or anything in the past, present, or future, sent His Son to die for you so that He can enjoy your company forever, your worth is beyond description. We can eagerly accept His grace, enfolding ourselves in His arms like a lamb in a shepherd's embrace. What joy and peace that gives, and what soothing to a soul wracked with self-doubt and feelings of imperfection.

I can tell you from personal experience of walking with God for over fifty years that He is the Lover of my soul. I have found

Him to be faithful in every situation. When someone is critical of what I am doing or I feel that I have let others down, His grace is something I can rely on for comfort.

I can tell you, from personal experience of walking with God for over fifty years, that He is the Lover of my soul.

Each of us has personal struggles that we can't seem to conquer. For some, it is perfectionism, the idea that everything you do and say has to meet a high standard. For others, it may be comparing yourself with others and coming up short. Or perhaps you have grown up in an atmosphere of criticism and harsh words that has left your soul shriveled and bare. It doesn't matter where your inner inadequacies come from; God's grace is greater than them all.

When you have symptoms of an illness, you make an appointment, go to the doctor, explain your symptoms, and ask for his professional diagnosis. With the information you give your heavenly Doctor, He makes the perfect diagnosis and prescribes what you should do to improve or eliminate the symptoms. When you come to Christ and accept His grace, you are healed from the pain you carry. When symptoms surface, you are free to go immediately to the Holy Spirit and find just the right remedy to overcome your challenge.

Living in Grace

Well-known pastor and theologian Donald Barnhouse tells a story that gives us a beautiful picture of the grace of God:

Years ago in France, as I watched a potter at work, He asked me if I would like to try my hand at making something. So I took a lump of clay, wet my hands, shaped the clay, and threw it against the wheel. As it began to turn, I pressed my hand against the clay, and it rose up into a pillar. Then I put my finger into the middle and made an opening.

I had formed a lovely vase with a flange at the bottom. Then it bellied out and narrowed to a neck. Thinking that it should be just a little narrower above the flange, I put my fingers there. Suddenly the vase broke.

Smiling, the potter took the same bit of clay and made a beautiful vase. Then he put it in his kiln to bake. When it came out, it was beautiful.

God works like that in our lives. We mar them but He makes them beautiful. When God takes a life deformed by sin and molds it into the image of Jesus Christ, all heaven rejoices. We are to the glory of His grace.[1]

In the rest of this section, we will be digging into the truths of God's grace. In the next chapter we will see how grace is given as a gift. Then we will explore how grace allows us to exchange the life we are now living for one that is truly satisfying. Last, we will find out the relationship between our guilt and God's grace.

Early in our ministry, my husband developed a simple way of sharing his faith in Christ with others. He called it "God's Plan," and it included spiritual "laws," or steps, for finding God's grace. (Eventually, this plan became *The Four Spiritual Laws*, a booklet Christians can use to tell others about the good news of Jesus Christ, which has sold billions of copies worldwide.) Each of the staff members of Campus Crusade would memorize the presentation to use with students or other people they met.

One morning at two o'clock, several women and I were in a downstairs room of our home typing a draft of "God's Plan" to be used for a presentation the following day. Bill had gone to bed because he faced a full schedule in the morning.

Suddenly, he came running down the stairs, telling us that the first law had to be rewritten. Originally, the first law explained that people are sinful and need to repent before they can have a relationship with God. At that time that approach was common in Christian circles. But Bill wanted to begin with an emphasis on God's love because he felt this is what draws people to God. In fact, he believed that God's love is the foremost principle of the universe. So the first law became "God loves you and has a wonderful plan for your life."

This law is not only true for the moment when you came to Christ and were forgiven of all your sins, but it is also the foundation for your Christian life. That's what makes our spiritual journey such an adventure of joy. God's love is the truth on which we can stake our lives.

God's grace and His love—we cannot separate them. They are one and the same. They are freely given to you, at this moment, just as you are. Accept God's grace, and allow Him to heal the woman within you.

FOUR

A Glorious Gift

Some years ago Penny lost her wedding ring when she took it off to wash dishes and it fell down the drain. Although she took apart the trap under the sink, she never recovered her ring. It was gone. In time she got used to the bare feeling on her finger, but she deeply regretted losing the one item that she valued most.

November was her fiftieth birthday, a milestone in her life. Her coworkers had a little party for her and gave her some sweet gifts. But the gift that made her cry was a surprise visit from her husband, who was holding a small package. Inside was a diamond ring shaped like a rose. She wept tears of joy.

Only those who know and love us well will discern the kind of gift that will touch our soul. You probably can think of a few gift-receiving experiences in your lifetime that have taken you to such an emotional high.

Another aspect of gift giving is how the item is wrapped. Gift wrap has taken on a new dimension in the last twenty years. The stationery industry has created so many options for making packages beautiful that it can become a major decision to select a gift bag or a box, the coordinated tissue lining, wrapping paper, and finally the ribbon and bow. I enjoy beautiful packaging, and I feel a little sad as I tear into a lovely gift and destroy the wrapping. Yet I never tire of opening gift packages. I receive more than my share from dear friends who give treasures I enjoy with delight.

When I read the story about Christ's birth and think about Mary wrapping baby Jesus in soft cloths, my heart rejoices to realize that the greatest gift ever given was wrapped quite simply, yet those wrappings held the source of humankind's redemption. Mary didn't have access to baby stores with elaborate color-coordinated blankets and booties, but I choose to believe that she was prepared with the softest of clothes for the newborn King. Then my mind moves from the image of those "swaddling" clothes to the wrappings left in the tomb when God's greatest gift was unwrapped of all the graveclothes and came forth as our Redeemer. Christ's resurrection was another gift unwrapped for us.

Nothing can compare to the magnificent glory of the gift of forgiveness in God's Son. Accepting that gift is the privilege of every person who believes. What do we receive when we accept God's gift? Think of it: not just forgiveness of sin, but purpose for living, the privilege of prayer, the indwelling of the Holy Spirit, adoption into God's family, joy of heart, power to cope, hope, peace, purpose, and assurance of eternal life. Everything we have and are is a gift from God made known in Jesus Christ.

You have already accepted God's gift of Jesus Christ into your life, but what now? A gift is only as good as the use to which you put it. If someone gives you a gorgeous bouquet of flowers, it will serve no purpose unless you place it where you can enjoy its beauty. The gift will be useless if you pack it away in the garage.

While teaching a group of women how to share their faith, I chose a woman named Chris, who was not sure she was a Christian, to help me demonstrate the use of *The Four Spiritual Laws* booklet. We read through the material until we came to the place where the reader is directed to receive Christ by faith. I asked her if she would like to do this. She affirmed that she believed everything I had shared, but she couldn't receive Christ because receiving Christ just couldn't be that easy. I changed my approach a couple of times, but her answer was the same.

You have already accepted God's gift of Jesus Christ into your life, but what now? A gift is only as good as the use to which you put it.

Only a few days before, I had returned from a trip to Egypt. I brought back an inlaid wooden box that was sitting on the coffee table. I asked Chris if she would receive a gift I wanted to give her. I showed her the box, explaining that I had bought it in Cairo to give someone, and she must be that someone. She agreed to accept the gift for the sake of the illustration.

I explained, "No, I want you to accept it as your own and to use the box."

She consented with delight.

Then I told her, "God offers you a far more valuable gift. Will you receive Christ just like you accepted my gift?"

She said yes and bowed her head in prayer to ask Christ into her life.

I explained, "Now, just as you will use the box, you need to apply your faith."

When we finished, the other women in the group hugged and embraced her warmly, welcoming her as a sister in Christ. She radiantly went on her way.

The next morning she greeted me by saying, "I'm using my box." She had grasped the truth of using God's gift of salvation.

God has so much to offer us if we will, by faith, use the gift He has given us. Just like the gift of His Son, His spiritual gifts are not wrapped with paper and ribbon but are oh so beautiful as we enjoy them daily.

The Gift of a Relationship

One of the gifts we receive when we enter God's family is an intimate relationship with him. Isn't that hard to imagine? God, who threw the stars into place with a word and who designed the DNA of all living creatures, actually wants to walk and talk with us! If the queen of England called and said she was stopping by my house for a cup of tea, I'd be floored. But the fact that God came to live within me is a far greater honor.

A good friend of mine, Chuck Swindoll, presents a wonderful example of the relationship God wants to have with us. He tells the story of Anne Lindberg, who married the indomitable Charles Lindberg, the famous aviator. Anne's father was the ambassador to Mexico when she met the adventurous young man who was flying from place to place promoting aviation. Crowds lined up to see him because he had won forty thousand dollars for being the first to cross the Atlantic by air. Chuck Swindoll tells us:

The strong pilot and the shy princess fell deeply in love. . . . When she became Mrs. Charles Lindberg, Anne could have easily been eclipsed by her husband's shadow. She wasn't, however. The love that bound the two together for the next forty-seven years was tough love, mature love, tested by triumph and tragedy alike. They would never know the quiet comfort of being an anonymous couple in a crowd. The Lindberg name didn't allow that luxury. Her man, no matter where he went, was news, forever in the limelight . . . clearly a national hero. But rather than becoming a resentful recluse or another nameless face in a crowd of admirers, Anne Morrow Lindberg emerged to become one of America's most popular authors, a woman highly admired for her own accomplishments.[1]

Anne describes her marriage and career in this way: "To be deeply in love is, of course, a great liberating force and the most common experience that frees. . . . Ideally, both members of a couple in love free each other to new and different worlds. I was no exception to the general rule. The sheer fact of finding myself loved was unbelievable and changed my world, my feelings about life and myself. I was given confidence, strength, and almost a new character. The man I was to marry believed in me and what I could do, and consequently, I found I could do more than I realized."[2]

Swindoll comments on Charles and Anne's dynamic relationship:

Charles did believe in Anne to an extraordinary degree. He saw beneath her shy surface. He realized that down in her innermost well was a wealth of wisdom, a deep profound, untapped reservoir of ability. Within the security of his love she was freed—released—to discover and develop her own capacity, to get in touch with her own feelings, to cultivate her own skills, and to emerge from that cocoon of shyness a beautiful, ever-delicate butterfly whose presence would enhance many lives far beyond the perimeter of her husband's shadow. He encouraged her to do her own kind of flying and he admired her for it. . . .

Make no mistake about it, this lady was inseparably linked in love to her man. In fact, it was within the comfort of his love that she gleaned the confidence to reach out, far beyond her limited shy world.

We're talking roots and wings. A husband's love that is strong enough to reassure yet unthreatened enough to release. Tight enough to embrace yet loose enough to enjoy. Magnetic enough to hold, yet magnanimous enough to allow for flight . . . with an absence of jealousy as others applaud her accomplishments and admire her competence. Charles, the secure, put away the net to Anne, the shy, so she could flutter and fly.[3]

Do you realize that God describes our relationship with Jesus as that of a bride and groom? We, as the worldwide church, are the bride. Jesus is the groom. "You husbands must love your wives with the same love Christ showed the church. He gave up his life for her to make her holy and clean, washed by baptism and God's word. He did this to present her to himself as a glorious church without a spot or wrinkle or any other blemish. Instead, she will be holy and without fault" (Ephesians 5:25-27).

Our wedding ceremonies, in which the bride comes in dressed in a spotless white gown, reflect this scriptural truth. But in the spiritual sense, Jesus Christ not only agrees to love us forever, He is also the One who frees us so that we can come before God without a spot or blemish. Our sins are forgiven; we are dressed in a white robe of righteousness. That means that our acceptance before God is not dependent on how we live but on the sacrifice Christ made. As the bride of Christ, we can have a loving, close, warm relationship with Him.

Even if the queen of England came to my house for tea, she and I would not have an intimate conversation. She'd sit on the edge of her chair, sip her tea, and make small talk. I'd be so nervous that I probably would spill tea on her lap when I poured! But that's not how we come before God. Of course, we must maintain our sense of awe that we are talking to and walking with the God of the universe who deserves all praise. At the same time, He invites us to bring every care we have and place it upon His shoulders. Just as in the relationship between Charles and Anne, Jesus gives us roots in His Word for security and wings to fly for our enrichment. Sometimes the truth of this relationship just makes me shout for joy!

The Gift of Total Acceptance

Because God loves us so much, another gift He gives us is complete acceptance of our weaknesses and limitations. In fact, these are vehicles through which He works in us and receives glory.

Let me tell you about Linda. In the first letter I received from her, she asked my suggestions for helping high school students improve the moral fiber of their community. She was a teacher who worked closely with teenagers. After that, Linda wrote regularly to tell me about her work and the exciting opportunities she had to see many students come to know Christ.

Because God loves us so much, another gift He gives us is complete acceptance of our weaknesses and limitations.

After hearing from Linda for three years, I learned that she had volunteered to care for the children during Campus Crusade staff training. I eagerly anticipated meeting her. We talked over the telephone and arranged a time for us to meet. Before that day, however, a friend came to me and said, "Linda doesn't think you'll like her after you see her."

I suspected from her comment that Linda might have a physical handicap and was worried about my reaction to her.

Later that week we were introduced in person. As she talked, she anchored her elbow in one hand to hold her chin steady as she tried to speak coherently. It was a joyful experience for both of us as we conversed. Then, as she turned to leave, I recognized the spastic condition of her frail body. Seldom have I been more moved than when I met Linda and realized the tremendous influence she had for Christ in spite of her physical limitations.

What gave this woman the purpose and radiance she obviously experienced? What motivated her to strive for fulfillment and accomplishment? I knew that Linda would answer those questions without hesitation: Jesus Christ had given her real life and acceptance. Through her, He was touching many lives.

You may feel that you are unworthy to be used by God to influence your corner of the world for Him. Let me emphasize that God's gift of Jesus Christ includes total acceptance of who you are. Don't ever think that your Husband is critical about your personality, your physical self, or your mental abilities. He does not discriminate. Every person on earth is precious to Him. And those who are part of His bride, the church, have an open invitation to converse intimately with Him.

Out of the Shadows

Sometimes, however, we let shadows come between the Lord and us. In order to cast a shadow, some substance must be opaque enough to block the rays of the sun. Psychological and spiritual shadows are far more subtle. Only the person living behind them knows they exist. They may be the result of a parent relationship that was based on performance, or a feeling of inadequacy carried from childhood because of a cruel remark from a schoolmate. The origin of the shadow is not nearly as important as how we handle it. Spiritual shadows come when we allow our minds to measure our spirituality by someone else. We observe a person who seems to always have an up-to-date testimony of leading someone to Christ or who has just done the most noble deed of kindness. Then we look at our own spiritual lives and realize that we haven't taken the time to read the Bible, pray, or share our faith consistently. The shadow looms heavily overhead and discouragement is soon to follow.

There is another shadow that clouds the lives of many

women. Surveys reveal that the number one problem women identify is loneliness. When I first read that comment, I found it difficult to understand. Our mobility allows us to move about so freely and with so many women actively involved in the market-place, it seems impossible that loneliness could plague the hearts and minds of American women. Yet when a life is not centered in the knowledge of eternal life and the promise of God to never leave us or forsake us, an underlying sense of loneliness is under-standable.

It should not come as a shock to learn that many Christian women experience a period of failure and defeat after their conversions. They almost despair of ever finding complete free-dom. But after searching for some time, with relief and joy they come into a new understanding of the grace of the indwelling Christ that transformed their lives. They begin to open the gifts that God has given them.

Are you still opening the package that you received the day you asked Jesus Christ to be your Savior? Or have you put it in the "garage" where you can't see it?

Perhaps at some time you received a Christmas present that was wrapped so that you discovered one box inside another. As you unwrapped one gift, you found another nestled inside. That's what our entire Christian life resembles. We unwrap one grace gift after another. As we grow in God's Spirit, He reveals more of His love to us. As we get deeper into His love, our rela-tionship with Him becomes more intimate. As we get closer to Him, we become more aware of His love for us. This is an amaz-ing cycle that never ends.

I encourage you to feel totally secure in God's grace. It's like being in the center of a lake when a forest fire is raging around you. You will feel coolness in the midst of the extreme heat of life. You will rest when the world around you is in turmoil. You can talk to God when no one else will listen.

Aren't you glad you made the decision to follow Christ? I sure am, especially as I unwrap His gifts to me day by day!

FIVE
A Surrendered Lifestyle

*W*hen Bill and I were married, his friends became my friends. Every place we went, he was very considerate and introduced me to people. But often I would find that he was involved in private conversations, projects, or committee meetings that did not concern me. I often spent long hours just waiting for him to finish his business.

One Sunday morning after we had been married for two years, a couple sought Bill's counsel and asked to speak to him privately after church. They were very cordial and polite to me, but I felt ignored as they left me and went to another room. After one hour had passed into two, and two into three, Bill finally appeared. He was apologetic, but I felt so rejected and unable to contribute that I could only respond with tears. Although Bill was very loving, it took me a little time to regain my composure.

Bill and I had to come to an understanding about our difference, so that afternoon after finishing dinner, Bill suggested that we prayerfully consider and then list on paper what we personally desired and wanted to accomplish in our lifetimes. Highly motivated to set my goals and work toward mutual goals that would help us avoid incidents such as the one earlier in the day, I went into one room to seek God's direction while Bill went into another.

Several hours later we compared our lists. Both of us began with the desire to have the Holy Spirit guide us and to have our lives, separately and together, bring honor and glory to God. Bill went on to express the hope that his personal ministry would help change the world. Then every item following those two concerned God's direction in his personal life and ministry.

My list included a desire to have two to four children and a house modest enough to entertain a person from skid row but elegant enough to entertain the president of the United States. I thought we needed at least two automobiles—I suggested mine could be a blue Ford, the least expensive car at that time. Since we were listing what we wanted, I decided that I might as well be specific.

Although my list included immediate material concerns, the opportunity to consider what I really wanted and what God had for me was a significant time because it was then that I began to really set my thoughts on the riches, treasures, and joys of heaven. After we realized God's desires for us, it was as if the struggle for material possessions, prestige, and honor were all cast aside. That day Bill and I signed a contract with the Lord in which we relinquished all claims to our lives. Approximately twenty-four hours later, God gave us the vision for Campus Crusade for Christ. It is doubtful that God would have entrusted us with the ministry had we not first made a full surrender of our lives to Christ. The full surrender brought us to a place of total dependence upon the Holy Spirit for direction and strength to maintain our commitment.

Starting a New Lifestyle

God wants us to willingly present ourselves completely to Him. Romans 12:1 says, "Therefore, I urge you, brothers, in view of God's mercy, to offer your bodies as living sacrifices, holy and pleasing to God—this is your spiritual act of worship" (NIV). Did you notice that Paul uses the word "urge"? This commitment is essential to the way we live in Christ. When we think of God's mercy, what He has done for us in forgiving our sins and coming to live within us, our response should be to kneel before Him in all humility and offer ourselves completely to Him. Christ offered His life for us. In return, we must become a living offering for Him.

After we realized God's desires for us, it was as if the struggle for material possessions, prestige, and honor were all cast aside.

As long as we resist God's will and hold on to former sinful habits like bitterness, discouragement, and anger, God cannot work in our lives. But when we submit to Him and thank Him, we learn the lessons that He wants us to know. This is a giant step toward becoming fulfilled as a Christian and as a woman.

As Romans 12:1 points out, surrendering ourselves to God is our spiritual worship. Many Christians hesitate to present their bodies to God, fearful that God might have a plan that would not be to their liking. But we were made for God, and we cannot operate properly without Him. Think of what would happen if a driver put water instead of gasoline into her gas tank. The car wouldn't run! Only when she pumps in gasoline will the car be able to function. That's the way we are too. We must be filled with the desires and Spirit of God to operate properly.

Romans 12:2 adds, "Do not conform any longer to the pattern of this world, but be transformed by the renewing of your mind. Then you will be able to test and approve what God's will is—his good, pleasing and perfect will" (NIV).

We cannot take the step in verse 2 until we have surrendered ourselves to God. He gives us the freedom and knowledge to choose His will. Our part is to trust and obey Him and make ourselves available to do what He asks of us. God doesn't want us to strive in our own power to be like Him. He doesn't need our help. He wants us to let Him live His life in and through us. He makes this possible through the Holy Spirit who lives within us as we daily surrender to Him. (We will discuss the Holy Spirit's role in the Christian adventure in a later chapter.)

The chief characteristic of this world is selfishness. Everyone wants his own way. But God wants us to be fashioned after Him and not this world. God has made us free moral agents with the ability to make our own choices. When Paul uses the word *will* in Romans 12:2, He means a plan or blueprint. For God's plan to be worked out in our lives, we must present ourselves to Him for His total control.

Taking the Step of Surrender

I love the way Steve Lawson, in his book *Absolutely Sure,* describes the depth of the commitment that every Christian needs to make in presenting himself to God:

It was the spring of 1519, and the famous explorer Hernando Cortes had secured eleven ships and seven hundred men from the governor of Spain. Armed with this sizable armada, he set sail from Europe to discover the New World.

His transatlantic voyage took several months, and upon his arrival in Vera Cruz, Cortes performed two dramatic acts that left an indelible impression upon his men. First he planted the flag of Spain upon the sandy beach of the New World, claiming this land for his sovereign. Then he issued a command that shook his men to the depths of their souls.

The message was clear: there was no turning back. All ties to their past were severed. No possibility existed of returning home. Their only option was to press forward into the uncharted interior of Mexico and meet whatever might come their way. Before their watching eyes, Cortes ordered all eleven ships anchored in the bay to be burned.

This is the commitment we must make to Jesus Christ. When we come to faith in Him, we plant the cross within our heart and stake a claim for our newly enthroned King. All escape routes leading back to the world are severed. All ties to our past way of life are burned. This step of faith breaks our old loyalties and establishes a new allegiance to Christ. The old has passed away; new things have come.[1]

Have you already made that decision? The most important step of your life is when you not only receive Christ as your Savior but also surrender your all to Him. This decision must be made in all seriousness and with a heart of love for God.

If you have not yet done this, I encourage you to do so now.

The following is a prayer you could adapt in making your decision:

> *Dear heavenly Father,*
>
> *I am so glad that I am Your child and that You have adopted me into Your eternal family. I can't express how grateful I am that Your Son, Jesus Christ, paid the penalty for all my sins when He died on the cross. Because of Your love and sacrifice for me, I want to give back everything I am and ever will be to You. I present my body to You as a living sacrifice for Your glory. I want to accomplish Your will and to grow to be more like Your Son, Jesus.*
>
> *In Jesus' name,*
> *Amen.*

As I look back on my life, I wonder what would have happened if I had followed my own desires instead of signing that contract with God. Through the years I have learned that you can never outgive God. He has blessed me in every way: ministry, relationships, faith beyond what I could have imagined. Even materially Bill and I owned little but enjoyed much. One thing I know for sure: I would not be the fulfilled and joyful woman that I am now. Only God could have made that change in me.

Living a Surrendered Life

What does this surrender of yourself to God mean to your daily life? You may be a young mother trying to find balance in your schedule as you drop off one child at school and devote your day to a baby who requires your constant care. The real-life, flesh-and-blood woman you are may spend countless hours serving your family, but at some point your responsibilities become burdensome rather than joyful. If you are a career woman with a family, you have different challenges. No matter what your situation—homemaker, career woman, grandmother, or single young woman—we all have common needs. The Creator has designed us with a spiritual nature that can only be at peace when we have surrendered everything we are to Jesus Christ. Understanding this truth was a process for me, and this process had some glitches that required penetrating looks into my life and the values I held dear.

What I learned through the many experiences of daily life was the practical reality of turning my hurts, desires, wants, and emotional ups and downs over to God as an ongoing act that flowed from my first surrender to God. When I did, I learned a valuable truth: God does not want us to work for Him, nor does He want to be our helper. Rather, He wants to do His work in and through us. Knowing this has brought about the most marvelous experience of a moment-by-moment walk in fellowship with Him.

God does not want us to work for Him, nor does He want to be our helper. Rather, He wants to do his work in and through us.

Bernard Christenson writes, "The living of the spiritual life is not the decision of a moment; it is the achievement of a lifetime, enabled and empowered by the Holy Spirit." It was only as I realized happiness depended upon my relationship to God and my availability to Him that my attitude changed. It didn't matter how much work I had to do, how much confusion flew around me, or how people treated me. Jesus was my source of joy, energy, and power. All I had to do was renew my surrender to Him whenever I found myself straying from God's will. Then I found that God would give me a contented heart. Hallelujah! This works! I've experienced it, as have millions of others who have surrendered all to Jesus.

Developing a Surrendered Lifestyle

I sometimes get a chuckle out of the way the devout Christian life is described by unbelievers. They imagine the Christian woman to be characterized by drab, unattractive dress, a person with no joy who lives a self-denigrating life. Others observe the professing Christian who attends church on Sunday but gives little evidence of commitment to Christ during the week and therefore conclude that "religion" doesn't make a difference. After all, her lifestyle and actions are much the same as women who have no time for God.

But these stereotypes are poles apart from the vibrant woman who has surrendered her life to God. I rejected those images long ago and determined to turn from that which was just form and ritual.

Think of the lifestyle of Jesus. Do form, ritual, and shallow commitment describe His way of living? Absolutely not! Jesus spent time with people, loving them and serving them. He didn't become irritated with the crowds but invited their presence and patiently taught them. What did He do with His disciples? He spent time with them, showed them God's nature, saw to their needs. Was Jesus unhappy or crabby or resentful? No, He gloried in accomplishing His Father's will.

The Christian lifestyle is not one of legalistic do's and don'ts, but one that is positive, attractive, and joyful. Compare the experiences of the disciples with those of the Pharisees, who tried to do God's will in their own strength and wisdom. The Pharisees always seemed to be waiting around trying to catch someone breaking their religious laws. Jesus and the disciples always seemed to be touching people's hearts and lightening their burdens. There's no doubt about which group of people experienced the true adventure!

But one aspect of the Christian life can defeat us even after we have surrendered our all to God. That is the burden of guilt. Many of us carry a heavy load of guilt and shame. In our next chapter we will explore the plan God has to deal with this problem to restore the woman within.

SIX

Giving Up on Guilt

$\mathcal{W}$hen women are asked what troubles them most, guilt feelings are frequently at the top of the list. A friend recently said to me that she feels guilty when she doesn't feel guilty. Doesn't that sound silly? Of course it does when we hear it, but the pressures from our culture to be "superwomen" set us up for feelings of inadequacy. Our expectations of what life should be and how those we love should respond may be set so high that there is no way we can be pleased with life—which leads to guilty feelings.

Much of our guilt is self-imposed rather than based on justifiable criteria. When the woman within you is committed to Jesus Christ, you will not automatically be free of self-imposed guilt or of the only real guilt that counts—sin guilt. So two guilt problems plague us: false guilt and real guilt. Let's get to the source of our guilty feelings so we can learn how to deal with them.

The Source of Guilt

Many Christians do not understand the biblical promise that they can live above the bondage of sin. Let me explain. God created all of us to have fellowship with him, but Adam and Eve, by their own stubborn self-wills, broke the relationship with God and fell into sin's clutches. Paul tells us in Romans 5:12-17:

> When Adam sinned, sin entered the entire human race.
> Adam's sin brought death, so death spread to everyone, for
> everyone sinned. . . . What a contrast between Adam and
> Christ, who was yet to come! And what a difference between
> our sin and God's generous gift of forgiveness. For this one
> man, Adam, brought death to many through his sin. But
> this other man, Jesus Christ, brought forgiveness to many
> through God's bountiful gift. And the result of God's
> gracious gift is very different from the result of that one
> man's sin. For Adam's sin led to condemnation, but we
> have the free gift of being accepted by God, even though we
> are guilty of many sins. The sin of this one man, Adam,
> caused death to rule over us, but all who receive God's
> wonderful, gracious gift of righteousness will live in
> triumph over sin and death through this one man, Jesus
> Christ.

Because of Adam's sin, humankind incurred guilt and a Savior became necessary. So in God's time, Jesus Christ came to earth to be born of a virgin. God became flesh and blood so that through His own death He might destroy the one who has the power of death over us—Satan. God made a way through His Son that we might be bought by His blood out of our hopeless condition of sin and guilt.

Watchman Nee, in *The Normal Christian Life*, writes:

Our salvation lies in looking away to the Lord Jesus and in
seeing that the Blood of the Lamb has met the whole situation
created by our sins and has answered it. That is the sure foundation on which we stand. Never should we try to answer
Satan with our good conduct but always with the Blood. Yes,
we are sinful, but, praise God! The Blood cleanses us from
every sin. God looks upon the Blood whereby His Son has
met the charge, and Satan has no more grounds to attack. Our
faith in the precious Blood and our refusal to be moved from
that position can alone silence his charges and put him to
flight.[1]

Although our righteous position is firm in God's sight, we don't
always act as if we are the King's kids, and we disobey our
Father. Any believer who, because of sin, is out of fellowship
with God is miserable indeed. The Holy Spirit within is grieved,
and He convicts us of our wrongdoing through guilty feelings.
That conviction is the source of guilt. At
that point we have a decision to make: to
turn away from sin or to be miserable and
suffer the consequences of our continued
disobedience.

When a believer wants to be right with
God, she has an advocate with the Father,
Jesus Christ the righteous. Our Advocate
before the court of heaven appears in our
behalf. John writes, "My dear children, I am
writing this to you so that you will not sin.
But if you do sin, there is someone to plead

*We have a
decision to
make—to turn
away from sin or
to be miserable
and suffer the
consequences of
our continued
disobedience.*

for you before the Father. He is Jesus Christ, the one who pleases God completely" (1 John 2:1). Jesus himself pleads our cause. The One against whose blood we have sinned is our Advocate.

At the same time, Satan, the accuser of the brethren, may be present to witness against us. But when Jesus Christ pleads our case on the merit of His shed blood, Satan has no ground on which to stand.

The Role of Confession

The way to deal with any sin, and thereby address the problem of guilt, is to first confess it to God. He promises us in 1 John 1:9, "If we confess our sins to him, he is faithful and just to forgive us and to cleanse us from every wrong." We can call this "keeping short sin accounts" with him. Rather than hoarding up sinful acts, which interfere with my communion with God, I immediately confess each sin as the Holy Spirit brings it to my mind. This stops guilt in its path. Once the sin is sincerely confessed, guilt has no legitimate place in my life, so I can renounce it. In addition, confession helps me deal with other sin in my life. Best-selling author and pastor Max Lucado beautifully describes how this works in our lives:

> Confession does for the soul what preparing the land does for the field. Before the farmer sows the seed he works the acreage, removing the rocks and pulling the stumps. He knows that seed grows better if the land is prepared. Confession is the act of inviting God to walk the acreage of our hearts. "There is a

rock of greed over here Father, I can't budge it. And that tree of guilt near the fence? Its roots are long and deep. And may I show you some dry soil, too crusty for seed?" God's seed grows better if the soil of the heart is cleared.

And so the Father and the Son walk the field together; digging and pulling, preparing the heart for fruit. Confession invites the Father to work the soil of the soul. . . .

Am I overstating the case when I announce, "Grace means you don't have to run anymore!"? It's the truth. Grace means it's finally safe to turn ourselves in.[2]

Does Max Lucado's message reflect your desire to keep your sin-accounts short? If so, then when your slate is clean of sin through confession, any further guilt about that sin is false.

While Satan's accusations before God must cease against us because of the blood of Christ, he may attempt to plague our conscience. It is one of his tricks. Although upon our confession, God forgives and cleanses us, Satan delights in tormenting us. Has he ever said to you, "That was a terrible thing you did. You don't think God loves you now, do you?" He has accomplished his purpose if he has succeeded in getting your eyes off Christ and onto your sin. This is false guilt and needs to be denied. You can tell Satan to take a hike!

The Battle Within

Perhaps you are thinking that you haven't seen much evidence of victory over sin in your life. One reason many Christians struggle with sin bondage is that they don't realize the power they have in Christ. Salvation is a twofold gift: Jesus Christ died on the cross to purchase for humankind not only freedom from the *penalty* of sin (Romans 5:8-10) but freedom from the *power* of sin as well (Romans 6:6-7).

Picture the cross of our Lord as having two arms. On one arm are written the words "for our sins," and on the other arm "unto sin." On the cross, He died "for our sins" so that we might never have to know a life of eternal separation from God. At the same time, He also died "unto sin" so that we might never have to experience a life of constant defeat.

Yet so many born-again believers know only a one-armed cross. They believe that Christ died for their sins, but they do not realize that He died unto sin, breaking the power of sin in their lives. No wonder many grow discouraged because of repeated failures.

So many born-again believers know only a one-armed cross. No wonder many grow discouraged because of repeated failures.

Our failure comes from the fact that we are unprepared to face the battle. The daily problem of sin results in a war within. Paul struggled with the problem of withstanding temptation: "I don't understand myself at all, for I really want to do what is right, but I don't do it. Instead, I do the very thing I hate" (Romans 7:15). He longed for some new power to take over in his life and make real in his experience the desire of his heart. He voiced his failure when he said, "I know I am rotten through and through so far as my old sinful nature is concerned. No matter which way I turn, I can't make myself do right. I want to, but I can't" (Romans 7:18). Finally, in desperation he cried, "Oh, what a miserable person I am! Who will free me from this life that is dominated by sin?" (Romans 7:24).

Have you experienced what Paul is talking about? This unhappy condition comes from the conflict between the two natures resident in the born-again believer—the flesh and the Spirit (Galatians 5:17). The old nature, the flesh, remains unchanged—a sinful nature. It is just as incapable of doing good as it was before we became Christians. It lies in wait, looking for every chance to seize the moment and become the dominant force in our lives. At the same time, our spirit says, "No! Don't give in to what you know will displease God." We are like the poet Goethe who complained about how unfortunate it was that nature had made of him but one man since he possessed all the materials for both a rogue and a gentleman.

How can we live lives of victory instead of defeat? By identifying with Jesus Christ in His death, burial, resurrection, and ascension. In Romans 6:3, Paul asks, "Have you forgotten that when we became Christians and were baptized to become one with Christ Jesus, we died with him?" The Phillips version translates the next verse: "We were dead and buried with him in baptism, so that just as he was raised from the dead by that splendid revelation of the Father's power so we too might rise to life on a new plane altogether" (6:4).

We who have been baptized into Christ Jesus have been baptized into His death. When Christ died, we died. Baptism here refers to every believer's birthright, his union with Christ. This union with Christ accomplished two things: the life of Christ was implanted in us (the new birth), and the power of sin was broken for us. We can now look back to the Cross and say with Paul, "I have been crucified with Christ and I no longer live, but Christ lives in me. The life I live in the body, I live by faith in the Son of God, who loved me and gave himself for me" (Galatians 2:20, NIV).

The boundless grace of God's provision for us as believers in Jesus Christ has now been unfolded before our eyes. We see the cross with both arms. Jesus has already provided deliverance for us from this terrible bondage of sin. Now He commands us to do our part through an act of faith by considering ourselves "dead to sin and able to live for the glory of God through Christ Jesus" (Romans 6:11).

To make this truth real in our own daily experiences, we must by faith see ourselves as dead to the influence of our sinful nature. The big challenges are easy for us to recognize, but it is the little things that seem to trip us. The day-to-day attitude we display in our home reflects just how much control we have given to the Holy Spirit and how much influence we allow our old nature. When the frustrations of coping with all the demands on our time seem overwhelming and our physical and emotional strength is spent, what do we do? How can we find the spiritual stamina we so desperately need?

Here's the answer: As we count ourselves dead to sin, we must also count ourselves alive to God in Christ Jesus. In Ephesians 2:6 we read, "He raised us from the dead along with Christ, and we are seated with him in the heavenly realms—all because we are one with Christ Jesus." As we are identified with His death, so we are identified with His resurrection life. We set our hearts on Christ and open ourselves to the working of the Holy Spirit, and He fights and wins our battles for us!

One area I struggled with was having a negative attitude in my home. At those times my husband, who was not only my best friend but also my minister and counselor, helped remind me that my disposition was not the most pleasing to him or to the family. Sometimes I came to my own defense, while at the same time I knew in my heart that he was right. That's when I had to confess and reaffirm that I am dead to that sin and alive in Christ. Now I ask God to handle my attitude through the power of His Holy Spirit living in me. You would not believe what a difference that choice makes in me and in my home!

The Bible tells us that sin is no longer our master (Romans 6:14), for we are not under law, which says "do," but under grace, which says "done." Grace is not partly man's work and partly God's work. Grace is wholly God's work; all we need to do is to receive it by faith as God's gift.

But sometimes we thwart God's grace by having a hidden agenda of sin. Because our hearts are so deceitful, at times we don't even realize what we are hiding from God. Next, we will examine these hidden agendas and the importance of dealing with them immediately.

> The Bible tells us that sin is no longer our master (Romans 6:14), for we are not under law, which says "do," but under grace, which says "done."

SEVEN

A Hidden Agenda

$\mathcal{H}$ave you heard the story of the little boy who tried to cover his sin? He lived in the South on a farm where his father grew delicious watermelons. As the melons began to ripen, his father said, "Son, you may have all the watermelon you can eat, but I do not want you to pick even one without my supervision."

"Okay, Dad," the boy replied.

But one day, in the cool of the morning, he decided just to walk through the patch and examine a few. He thumped a couple of them as he had seen his father do, and then he found one that he knew was just right for eating. It was cold, too, just the way he liked his melon.

He gave a hasty look toward the house; no one was in sight. Quickly he picked up the forbidden fruit and ran down by the creek, where he ate watermelon until he could hold no more. He hurriedly buried the remains in the sand, covering all evidence of his disobedience.

Sometime later the father delighted the boy by telling him to get his rod and they would go fishing. They started off in a merry mood, but as they came to the creek the father looked down and then stopped. Turning to his son he said, "What is the meaning of watermelon vines growing here?"

The lad hung his head and confessed his sin.

Then the father said, "Son, let this be a lesson to you. You can never cover your sin. You thought you had covered yours successfully, but you see it can't be done. Your sin has found you out."

We are warned in Proverbs 28:13: "People who cover over their sins will not prosper. But if they confess and forsake them, they will receive mercy." Because of the root of sin that dwells in us (our old sin nature), we are more ready to cover our sins than to abandon them. God's promise of mercy is to those who both confess and forsake their sin. Chrysostom describes the response we need to take when we recognize our hidden agenda: "I say not to thee, make a parade of thyself, nor yet, accuse thyself in the presence of others. Before God confess these things."

Every Christian should be eager to recognize any habit of sin that the Holy Spirit reveals and upon confession to trust the Spirit to put it out of her life. As we remember from reading 1 John 1:9, when we confess our sin, God not only forgives but also cleanses us from all defilement of sin. This word *cleanses* is in the *aorist* tense in Greek, the original language of the New Testament, denoting a thing done once. This indicates that known sin in the life of a believer is not to be a continuing act. Saints do not knowingly sin and keep on sinning over and over.

If there is something you know to be wrong, yet you have a certain liking for it, ask the Holy Spirit to help you see your bad habit as God does. If you are honest in your desire, a real hatred for the forbidden thing will replace the longing you once had for it.

Our Father's Justice

If we don't turn away from our habits of sin, we will suffer consequences. When we received Christ as Savior, we began a new relationship with God. No longer were we lawbreakers facing a judge, we became children of our heavenly Father, and He began dealing with us as such. Therefore, we are not punished as lawbreakers; we are chastened as children.

Perhaps you have known the pain of the chastening hand of the Father. I know I have, and it has not been pleasant. The Lord diligently prunes and molds our character to conform us into Christ's image. This is true whether we are in the public eye of ministry leadership or are a mother who is training little lives to serve God. We all have positions that can be detrimental to others if we don't reflect God's nature. Sometimes God's work in our lives is painful, and at those times I don't always want to accept God's will.

But while chastening is always difficult, if we look to God for the lesson we should learn, we will see spiritual fruit. "Now obviously no 'chastening' seems pleasant at the time: it is in fact most unpleasant. Yet when it is all over we can see that it has quietly produced the fruit of real goodness in the characters of those who have accepted it" (Hebrews 12:11, Phillips).

As soon as a difficulty arises in our lives, the first question we should ask ourselves is: Do I have a hidden sin agenda that is causing me to suffer for my spiritual disobedience? Not all trials and hard circumstances

While chastening is always difficult, if we look to God for the lesson we should learn, we will see spiritual fruit.

are brought by God's chastening, but if we get into the habit of examining our lives when things go wrong, we will be able to determine the times when God is trying to draw our attention to a problem in our lives. And certainly, if the problem has its root in a sin that we are harboring, we can be sure that God is allowing the difficulty to purify us of our wrong attitudes and actions. Then we can deal with it according to biblical principles.

Turning It Around

We have to live with this fact: our sin nature will always try to defeat us. Have you ever said something and immediately thought, *Why did I say that?* Most of us have. That is the old self. If you have, don't waste time trying to figure out a way to avoid doing it again. Living in this world will always be a challenge. Deal immediately with your sin and guilt each time it causes you problems. Don't hide your sin with excuses or rationalizations.

Consider some areas that trip up many people:

REBELLIOUS ATTITUDE

Do you have something within you that rebels when given orders? If so, you may correctly label that attitude as the "sinful nature." It hates to be told what to do. It wants its own way with no one to rule over it. We all inherited it from Adam and Eve, who chose to disobey God. We hate to be told when to get up or go to bed, what to wear or not wear, what to do or not do. Saul's rebellious nature kept him from becoming a great king in Israel. God rebuked him through the prophet Samuel: "What is more

pleasing to the Lord: your burnt offerings and sacrifices or your
obedience to his voice? Obedience is far better than sacrifice.
Listening to him is much better than offering the fat of rams"
(1 Samuel 15:22). Make obedience your goal.

FEELINGS OF UNWORTHINESS

The sinful nature may try to convince us that we are not worthy
of God's love and blessings. In a cry for reassurance, we may
denigrate ourselves in the hope of receiving praise from others.
However, this attitude keeps us from finding our identity in
Christ and relying on the Holy Spirit.

Do you occasionally glory in being the one who has to bear
the brunt of everything? Do you wallow in a martyr complex?
Perhaps you feel as if you are the one who gets the "raw deal,"
who never gets a good "break." Nothing is ever just right: if only
this thing or that thing could have been different. If only, if only.
Maybe you are a person who would never lose your temper or
speak a cross word, but you are easily offended. Of course, you
generally keep it hidden, but, oh, what a long memory you have!

BEING SELF-CENTERED

When we become self-centered, we begin to punctuate all our
conversation with the words *me, my,* and *I*. It is that "I" that urges
us to say, "Oh, yes, that reminds me of the time when I. . . ."

No one likes to think of herself as self-centered. Ask yourself
this question: When you look at a group picture that includes
you, who do you see first? Do you run your eye along and then
exclaim, "Oh yes, here I am in the second row"? Notice how

easily you lose interest in the conversation of others if you or your problems are not the center of the discussion. Also, think about how unimportant you consider a public issue if it does not concern you or your own affairs.

These sinful attitudes are our enemy. You can deny them by choosing obedience and joy!

Winning the Battle

Some time ago a lovely Christian woman took exception to how the Bible instructed her to count herself as dead to her sin of a bad temper. She had kept her temper in check for quite some time and felt that she had pretty well mastered it, but she was really running on self-effort.

Then she studied God's Word with an open mind and asked the Holy Spirit to instruct her on God's method of dealing with the works of the flesh. In doing this, she relinquished control of her own behavior and turned her life's control center over to God.

In a few weeks she had a glowing testimony. She had never realized the strain under which she had lived. When trying to manage her own weakness in the flesh, she had to be constantly alert in case something might cause her to lose her temper. But when she counted herself as dead to sin and alive in Christ Jesus, she was set free. With a radiant face she said, "How blessed it is to know that my old master cannot compel obedience from me as his slave, for death has broken the bond. I'm dead, praise God, I'm dead!"

Who will rule the woman within you? Will you succumb to

guilt and sin, or will you yield your total being to the influence of God's Spirit?

When I think about the word *yield*, I relate it to a yield sign on the road. The action of stopping or pausing long enough to know whether or not I can move into traffic is a good picture of what I need to do every time I start to take control of my life. I need to pause long enough to reflect on the possible consequences and realize that the Holy Spirit is in a better position to be in control of my life than I am.

We don't need to go through life second-guessing everything we say and do and living under a load of guilt, whatever its source. When the Holy Spirit dwells in us, we have a balance in our perspective, and even if we react negatively to a situation, He will guard our actions and bring us back to the point of true surrender.

As we have by faith said no to sin, so we should by faith say yes to God and set our minds on things above, where Christ is seated in the heavenlies. From there we see things from God's vantage point—circumstances, people, all that would hinder our enjoyment of the rest that God has provided for His people.

As we have by faith said no to sin, so we should by faith say yes to God and set our minds on things above, where Christ is seated in the heavenlies.

Let Go and Let God

Accepting God's grace really is simple, like the old adage "Let go and let God." It is letting go of our feelings of low self-worth and letting God show His love to us. And it is letting go of the desire to control our own lives and letting God "run the show." And it is letting go of all the sin and guilt built up over years of bad practices and letting God cleanse our spirits and keep us from sin.

This is something we can do! We can turn our backs on old ideas of working in our own strength to become worthy and instead rest in God's grace. We can reverse our hidden agenda and enjoy the blessing of God's agenda. What a contradiction this is in our frantic, do-it-all, have-it-all society!

Do you know what the secret is to resting in God's grace? Walking moment by moment in His Spirit. In the next chapter we will learn how this simple truth can revolutionize our lives.

EIGHT
A Person You Need to Meet

*A*fter I accepted Christ as my personal Savior, I was certain that my life would be perfect. But I soon realized that I was not seeing evidence of Christ working in me. What was I missing? I had heard about the work of the Holy Spirit, but I didn't really understand how His ministry related to me. I continued to be faithful with my prayer and Bible reading, sharing my faith, and taking an active part in my husband's ministry, but I was not seeing spiritual fruit in my life.

Just as a woman taking on a new role as a mother must learn how to parent, once my position in Christ was assured, I had to learn how to live according to scriptural principles.

At the time, Bill and I were hearing messages on revival and reports of wonderful victories for Christ. There had to be something more to this life in Christ, and I really wanted to know what it was.

A Gentle Nudging

During Bill's senior year at Fuller Seminary, God gave him a vision of what he was to do with his life. For five years he had obeyed God by leading ministry teams to jails, road camps, and churches, but he became increasingly concerned that very few teams were going to the college campus. He had been extremely active in student affairs, and now he felt that if someone had come to him with a positive Christian message when he was in college, he would have been interested. Yet no one had ever talked with him about Christ when he was a student.

Consequently, Bill organized a church team to go to the fraternities, sororities, and the various residential groups at USC and UCLA. The students responded, so we leased a home one block from the UCLA campus. Students poured into our home as if it were Grand Central Station.

The demands of every day kept me so busy that I subconsciously equated my busyness with commitment to Christ.

The demands of every day kept me so busy that I subconsciously equated my busyness with commitment to Christ. Here I was with a home filled with students and a husband who had boundless energy and more good ideas about expanding a ministry than we could accomplish in two lifetimes. Wasn't that enough?

That summer I attended a Christian women's retreat. During the conference, I was reminded of the scriptural principle that God demands obedience before He can give blessing. I read in Deuteronomy 11:27: "You will be blessed if you obey the commands of the Lord your God that I am giving you today."

The mention of obedience to God reminded me of some situations from years past. Although the matters seemed small and trivial, in several instances I had been impressed that I needed to apologize to some people, but I hadn't. So much time had passed since the incidents that I tried to brush off the gentle nudging I was feeling. But each time I desired to be used by God in someone's life, I would have a nagging thought that He couldn't really use me until I was obedient to what I knew He wanted me to do. Finally, while at the women's retreat, I sat down to write letters of apology.

Although the letters were written and sealed, I continued to struggle with mailing them. I was certain that the people receiving the letters were going to think I had become fanatical about insignificant issues, and I didn't want to be embarrassed. Finally, I went to the prayer chapel and spent time with God, asking Him to show me whether or not this was really what I had to do. I thought that perhaps my willingness to write the letters was enough, so now I didn't need to mail them. But I asked God to give me a way to know for certain.

On the way back to my room I overheard a conversation that related specifically to the situation for which I had written my letters. Right then I knew I had to mail them. I walked with confidence to the mailbox and put them in.

If you haven't guessed by now, that nudging was the Holy Spirit working in my life. In my spiritual immaturity I didn't understand the importance of responding to His voice as soon as I heard it. I had complete confidence in my salvation, but I did not understand that the Holy Spirit, the third person of the Trinity, had come into my life when I received Jesus Christ as my Savior and that He wanted to help me mature in my faith.

Like me, you may have felt that gentle nudging and ignored

it. It seems easier to pray about major decisions and seek God's guidance for direction when we face overwhelming challenges, but the truth about obedience to God is that it is not a "pick and choose" option. The real joy and true blessings that God promises are for when we obey Him in anything, anytime, anywhere. Obedience is a lifestyle. When we learn to live an obedient lifestyle, our perspective on every challenge becomes one of peace and confidence.

Soon, I received wonderful responses to the letters, which brought great relief to me. The incidents could now be forgotten. I had been obedient to God, and I was beginning to understand the presence and work of the Holy Spirit.

This was not a monumental event in the scheme of my life, but it brought out the reality that the Holy Spirit was alive in me. I could live moment by moment with the assurance that God would guide, and I would obey.

Knowing the Holy Spirit

If I asked you this question: "Do you know who the Holy Spirit is?" could you answer as confidently as if I asked, "Do you know who the Father and the Son are?" A noted theologian commented that more Christians are confused about the doctrine of the Holy Spirit than about any other Christian truth. So many know little more about Him than that He is part of the Godhead. He is the neglected, if not almost forgotten, person of the Trinity. Perhaps it's hard for you to think of the Holy Spirit as a person. If so, it may be because we generally associate a person with a body.

Personality, however, is not an attribute of body but of spirit. We must remember that the Trinity—the Father, Son, and Holy Spirit—is one God revealed in three persons.

The New Testament refers to the Holy Spirit more than 250 times. The Holy Spirit's attributes as well as His names give evidence that He is God. John 16:13 records, "When the Spirit of truth comes, he will guide you into all truth. He will not be presenting his own ideas; he will be telling you what he has heard. He will tell you about the future."

We experience no frustration when our minds are relying on Him. "You will keep in perfect peace all who trust in you, whose thoughts are fixed on you!" (Isaiah 26:3). The peace that passes understanding is ours by resting on Him, the omniscient One.

In 1947 Bill had a dramatic experience with the Holy Spirit when God gave him a great burden to help reach the world for Christ. In 1951 the Holy Spirit again dramatically touched Bill's life, resulting in his call to establish the ministry of Campus Crusade for Christ. His call became mine as well. A few years later Bill and I were vacationing on Balboa Island as guests of Dr. and Mrs. Charles E. Fuller of *The Old-Fashioned Revival Hour*. We were listening to messages on the Holy Spirit from Dr. J. Edwin Orr and reading books about the Holy Spirit by R. A. Torrey and other biblical scholars. We discovered a difference in the quality of life that people lead when they acknowledge the person and work of the Holy Spirit in their lives.

At that time there appeared to be a lack of clear definition about who the Holy Spirit is and how He manifests himself. Bill was driven to search the Scriptures and read every bit of information he could find to gain a scriptural understanding of what he had experienced and what he was hearing from different sources. He was also eager to put these biblical truths into words and teaching that would be transferable to Crusade staff and those whom they would influence. It was so obvious to both of us that if the world was to be reached for Christ, it would be the result of God's supernatural power released to and through people who had a desire to be supernaturally used by God.

We are greatly privileged to live in this period that was ushered in on the Day of Pentecost, forty days after Christ returned to heaven. Since then, the Spirit's ministry to believers has been vastly different from what it was in Old Testament times.

The Spirit could not come to permanently abide in believers until after the Lord Jesus returned to heaven: Jesus said, "It is actually best for you that I go away, because if I don't, the Counselor won't come. If I do go away, he will come because I will send him to you" (John 16:7). How thankful we should be that the Holy Spirit has come and clothed Himself with our humanity! The Holy Spirit is the One who dwells in us, guides us, and convicts us of sin. We couldn't live a holy life without His power. However, we cannot experience His power without being totally yielded and abandoned to Him.

What a comfort to know that God Himself is there in your life, available to meet every situation with you, that you are never left to face any problem alone!

Do you frequently thank God that the Holy Spirit is always in you as your constant companion? What a comfort to know that God Himself is there in your life, available to meet every situation with you, and that you are never left to face any problem alone!

Our Source of Power

Today the matter of power has captivated the minds of men. Governments are vying for it, believing that they must be at the forefront of the technological race to maintain their superiority.

While men strive ceaselessly to increase their might, God has something to say about a power the world cannot know. The Lord tells a people who were demoralized and beaten down by their enemies: "It is not by force nor by strength, but by my Spirit, says the Lord Almighty" (Zechariah 4:6).

The perfect life of Jesus Christ was lived in dependence upon the power of the Holy Spirit. If He, being God, so lived, certainly so should we! As Jesus explained to His disciples, "He is the Holy Spirit, who leads into all truth. The world at large cannot receive him, because it isn't looking for him and doesn't recognize him. But you do, because he lives with you now and later will be in you" (John 14:17).

Before Jesus ascended into heaven, He commanded those assembled with Him to wait for the coming of the Spirit. He promised, "When the Holy Spirit has come upon you, you will receive power and will tell people about me everywhere" (Acts 1:8). What was the result when that promise was fulfilled? Men who had been cowardly and afraid became bold and fearless witnesses. The uneducated spoke with such power that the listeners marveled and perceived that they had been with Jesus. Soon people were saying that these men were turning the world upside down. A new power in the person of the Holy Spirit had come to reside in them. That same power is in us today, for the Holy Spirit came to live within us the moment we trusted in Jesus Christ.

Later, Paul was surprised when he came to the city of Ephesus and discovered some disciples whose lives seemed to lack this supernatural power, so he asked them if they had received the Holy Spirit. They replied that they had never heard of the Holy Spirit. They knew Christ was the Lamb of God, but of the gift of the Holy Spirit they were completely ignorant. When they understood that Jesus Christ had been crucified, had risen, and had returned to heaven, they believed, and the Holy Spirit came to live in them, too.

Throughout life there will come times when we feel power-less. Any woman of adult children knows the ache of wanting to help her child realize he is making a wrong or unwise decision, yet she also realizes that an adult has the right to make his own decisions. If you find yourself in this situation, or in others that are hard to handle, it is a perfect opportunity for you to rely on the Holy Spirit to give you the strength to commit that child to God and pray earnestly for the outcome.

Being Filled with the Holy Spirit

Perhaps you are wondering what I mean when I say that the Holy Spirit lives in us but at times we may not appropriate His power. Let me explain the difference between being indwelled by the Holy Spirit and being controlled by the Holy Spirit. The Holy Spirit indwells every Christian from the moment of spiritual birth, but to be controlled by the Holy Spirit, you must, as an act of your will, completely surrender your life to live in obedience to Christ. This is the step that we talked about in an earlier chapter.

To live out this obedience daily, you must continue to be filled with the Holy Spirit by constant submission to Him. In Ephesians 5:18 we are commanded: "Don't be drunk with wine, because that will ruin your life. Instead, let the Holy Spirit fill and control you."

God never commands us to do anything that He does not give us the ability to do. He would never tell us to be filled with the Holy Spirit without enabling us to be filled. In the following chapter we will discuss how we can receive the fullness of the Holy Spirit by faith.

The placement of the verse commanding us to be filled with the Spirit is very interesting to me. Immediately after this portion, God speaks of relationships between husbands and wives, children and parents, and others. God is so practical. I've come to realize that unless the Holy Spirit controls our actions in our family situations, He is not likely to be in control at all. When we are filled with the Spirit, I believe that will be especially evident in our homes.

Being filled with the Holy Spirit does not mean that I will experience a high point of emotion or feel exhilarated spiritually or physically 100 percent of the time. Many people become disappointed when they learn that this is not true of the Spirit-filled life. They were hoping that they could do something to assure themselves of emotional highs all the time. Emotions come and go and cannot be relied upon; therefore, we should not allow feelings to affect our relationship with God. We must place our confidence in Him and in His promises. Though feelings are biblical and valid, it is our faith that makes the difference, not our feelings. As Romans 1:17 says, "The righteous will live by faith" (NIV), and Hebrews 11:6 adds, "It is impossible to please God without faith."

One remedy to the ups and downs of our emotional state is to walk in the Spirit by faith as a lifestyle. That's what we will learn about in the next chapter.

NINE

Being Aware of the Spirit

*W*hat impedes you from living a Spirit-filled life? Each of us would have different answers at various times in our lives. Sometimes it may be a certain temptation or the difficulties of a close relationship. At other times it may be uncontrolled emotions.

Often our physical health has an effect on our feelings. We may be extremely tired, and because we don't feel exhilarated, we may think we aren't filled with the Spirit. However, emotions are not a dependable guide. Our feelings may be simply due to our need for rest, more physical exercise, or a balanced diet.

Our attitudes are a much more reliable gauge of our relationship with God. I understood this clearly one afternoon years ago when I decided to mop the kitchen floor. I had happily gone about the task, but while the floor was drying, our younger son, Brad, came running into the house with a group of little boys trailing behind him. They wanted some milk, so Brad, without asking, decided he would get it. But while he was pouring the milk, he spilled it on my shiny floor.

When I saw the spill, I snapped loudly, "Get out of the kitchen! I just mopped the floor!"

All of the boys scurried out wide-eyed, scared because Brad's mother had spoken harshly. I felt terrible.

Now where was the Holy Spirit in this? He was still in my life, but He was not in control. I had exerted my will over His. My attitude was wrong.

The Throne Check

To avoid such incidents, Bill and I began to practice what we called the "throne check." It is based on the idea that in each life there is a throne, or control center. When the Holy Spirit controls our lives, our ego or self is dethroned. But self can take control at any moment, as it did in my floor-mopping incident. This doesn't mean the Holy Spirit leaves our lives; it means at that moment He isn't in control. We have taken Christ off the throne, thereby limiting the Holy Spirit's influence in our lives.

When Christ is in control, we experience harmony and peace.

Self-Directed Life

S – Self is on the throne
† – Christ dethroned and not allowed to direct the life
● – Interests are directed by self, often resulting in discord and frustration

Christ-Directed Life

† – Christ is in the life and on the throne
S – Self is yielding to Christ
● – Interests are directed by God, resulting in harmony with God's plan

When self is in control, we suffer with discord and frustration. The preceding two diagrams illustrate what I'm describing:

We taught this concept to our boys from early childhood, and we all practiced it. Every once in a while, when dispositions were not very pleasant, someone would ask, "Who is on the throne?" The person who was displaying selfish attitudes would then examine himself.

I remember vividly an incident when Brad was about four years old. I had decided to fix something special for the children's breakfast: a fried egg in a piece of toast with a hole in the center. I called this dish "egg in a bonnet."

Brad complained, "I don't like my egg like that, and I'm not going to eat it." He could manufacture tears in a second, and he did on this occasion. Bill was home, so I decided to allow him to deal with the situation.

Bill asked Brad, "Who is on the throne this morning?"

Brad responded in his preschool language, "The debil [devil] and me."

"Who do you want on the throne?"

"Jesus."

"What do you do?"

With the wisdom of a child, Brad responded, "Pray, 'Dear Jesus, please be on the throne, and help me eat this egg.'"

At four years old, Brad knew that putting Jesus on the throne of his life would allow him to overcome his own will and attitude, a lesson not every Christian has learned.

Later, a staff couple came to Arrowhead Springs for training. On this particular day Brad was running in the hotel with some other children. I had already told him not to run in the halls, so when he continued doing it, I stopped him and asked, "What is wrong with you? Is Jesus in control of your life? Do you want Him in control?"

At four years old, Brad knew that putting Jesus on the throne of his life would allow him to overcome his own will and attitude.

Brad simply said yes and stopped his rambunctious behavior.

The staff woman stopped in her tracks. She had given up a comfortable lifestyle to join the Crusade staff, yet she turned to me and said, "That's what is wrong with me." She explained that she wanted to control her own life, but God had different plans for her. What she needed to do was take herself off the throne and allow Jesus His rightful place.

Walking in the Spirit

Any sin in our lives can prevent the Holy Spirit from exercising His influence in us. This is why I have tried to develop the habit of keeping short accounts with God. As I walk closely with God, my acts of disobedience become less frequent. The more I obey Him, the more the Holy Spirit strengthens me to resist the temptation the next time.

One little area in my life continually gives me the opportunity to rely on the Holy Spirit to help me respond correctly. My husband was so devoted to the Lord and to serving Him that if it had not been absolutely necessary to eat, he would have completely forgotten about mealtime. Throughout most of our married life, I had to telephone him every evening to remind him to come home to dinner. Over the years I learned to look at the clock and gauge my call according to the time it took him to get his things together at the office and arrive home in time for dinner.

Only the power of the Holy Spirit could enable me to accept my husband's little idiosyncrasy and to make my call pleasant and even a special pleasure. But occasionally I decided he should be able to get home for dinner on his own initiative, so his forgetfulness irritated me.

Whenever I failed to call him with an attitude of patience and love, I knew what to do. My husband called the corrective action "Spiritual Breathing." In Spiritual Breathing we exhale by confessing our sins and inhale by appropriating God's promise of filling. I can claim God's marvelous promise of forgiveness and filling and know that He hears me. First John 5:14-15 says, "We can be confident that he will listen to us whenever we ask him for anything in line with his will. And if we know he is listening when we make our requests, we can be sure that he will give us what we ask for." After I exhale (confess the sin of impatience, or whatever sin I have committed), I inhale (appropriate by faith the fullness and control of the Holy Spirit in my life). As a result, I am able to continue in unbroken fellowship with God.

This illustration is more meaningful to me now than before. In later years, as Bill suffered with a breathing ailment that limited his strength, his lungs could not process oxygen as efficiently as before. This meant that we had to make some changes in our lives. He had to watch his schedule and also avoid certain activities.

I apply Bill's struggles with breathing to what happens if I don't exhale and clear the sin from my life. My spiritual strength is sapped, and I can't live the way God intended for me to live. I don't have the power to handle my circumstances, attitudes, and feelings. It's just so essential that I continually walk in God's power, filled by His Spirit, and allow Him to control every part of my life!

Dealing with Our Problems

Sometimes we take our eyes off of God because we are caught up in the fears and worries of this life. Yet this distraction makes our situation worse. When we focus on our problems rather than on walking in the Spirit, we become defeated.

As a city girl, Jeanne often went to visit cousins in the country. Her cousin Tom was just a year older, but he was much wiser in the ways of country living, and he enjoyed frightening Jeanne.

There was a swinging bridge stretching high above a rushing stream. Made of flexible steel cables and wooden slats, the bridge swayed with every step.

Whenever Jeanne went to visit, Tom always had something to show her—on the other side of the bridge! He would run across the bridge first. On the other end, he'd stand waiting. Yelling at Jeanne to hurry up, he'd grab the cables and shake them as hard as he could.

Not as sure-footed, Jeanne held on for dear life. Frozen with fright, she'd beg him to stop. The more she pleaded, however, the harder he laughed and taunted her.

Finally, Jeanne had had enough. She begged her dad to make Tom stop. But Jeanne's wise father told her she was the only one who could do that. He told Jeanne that when she was on the bridge she mustn't look down or yell, and she must keep walking. She could then focus her eyes on the great big tree in front of her to which the bridge cable was attached and walk toward it.

It sounded like great advice. So when Tom wasn't around, Jeanne practiced. She learned to walk across that bridge with confidence.

That's a good illustration of walking in the Spirit. At times it feels like someone's on the other side shaking the very cables of our lives. Sometimes we forget to Whom those cables are attached.

On those days—when your children are demanding and your husband isn't very understanding and your boss is crabby—look up and keep your eyes on Jesus. Focus on your relationship with God, and keep walking in the Spirit.

Being Transformed

Walking in the Spirit is the way we can give back to God for what He has done for us. Vernon Grounds tells a story that expresses this truth so well:

> One day a parishioner entered the study of F. B. Meyer, the well-known English preacher, in order to sign an important document. Lying on the pastor's desk was a fountain pen—an instrument regarded at the time as a remarkable invention.

The parishioner picked it up in order to write the signature, but Dr. Meyer restrained him. "Don't try using that," he said with a smile. "I call it my castaway. It refuses to be filled." Meyer's casual comment was a sermon in itself. He took 1 Corinthians 9:27 where Paul warns against the danger of being put aside as useless in God's service because we are not under the control of the Spirit—a castaway. He fused that text with Ephesians 5:18, "Keep on being filled with the Spirit." If we refuse to do that—or neglect to do that—we are not in danger of being cast away eternally, but we are in danger of being set aside as an instrument God cannot use.

Set aside. Shelved. Boxed away. Benched. What a tragic waste of potential! What a denial of all that God longs for us to do and be for the name of His Son. Let us cry out to our Father to so fill us with His Spirit that our lives brim over, spilling His life and joy like refreshing rain on a tired and cynical planet. And let us live in such a way that He will be pleased to grant our heart's desire.[1]

I have a deep joy today realizing that the decision I made to let Christ rule my life allowed me not to be set aside but to be set straight—straight on a path of the wonderful life of a true Christian woman. In Romans 12:2, Paul writes, "Don't copy the behavior and customs of this world, but let God *transform* you into a new person by changing the way you think" (emphasis added). The world lives for itself, for what it can gain; it strives for things that are transitory and purely selfish. But we have a completely different future. We are to be transformed by choosing God's plan for our lives and yielding to the control of the Spirit. As we do so, we are being changed in character and conduct in the process of becoming like our Lord Jesus Christ.

The Greek word for "transformed" is the same as that for "transfigured" when used about Christ on the Mount of Transfiguration. "There he was transfigured before them. His face shone like the sun, and his clothes became as white as the light" (Matthew 17:2, NIV). His character changed from one of humble servant to glorious deity. Here He gave outward expression to His inner life of glory. His transformation was a physical picture to us of what the Holy Spirit will do for our inner nature!

We find the same word used in 2 Corinthians 3:18: "We, who with unveiled faces all reflect the Lord's glory, are being transformed into his likeness with ever-increasing glory, which comes from the Lord, who is the Spirit" (NIV). This change is not a psychological one, nor is it one brought about by human effort. It is a continuing process of the Spirit's work in the life of a yielded believer. It is not by negative efforts of not doing this and not doing that but by obedience to the positive, by beholding the Lord.

This transformation is not gained in a moment. It is the ongoing work of the Spirit of God as we yield to Him, read His Word, meditate upon it, and submit to its teaching.

When we walk in the Holy Spirit, God can begin building in our lives the skills necessary to be an instrument for Him. All these skills, which we'll explore in the next section, come from the heart of the woman who is secure in God's love, living in His power.

PART 3

ACQUIRING OUR SKILLS

My child, listen to me and treasure my instructions. Tune your ears to wisdom, and concentrate on understanding. Cry out for insight and understanding. Search for them as you would for lost money or hidden treasure. Then you will understand what it means to fear the Lord, and you will gain knowledge of God. For the Lord grants wisdom! From his mouth come knowledge and understanding.

PROVERBS 2:1-6

The soul's house, that interior dwelling place which we all possess, for the upkeep of which we are responsible—a place in which we can meet God, or from which in a sense we can exclude God—that is not too big an idea for us. Though no imagery drawn from the life of sense can ever be adequate to the strange and delicate contacts, tensions, demands and benedictions of the life that lies beyond sense: though the important part of every parable is that which it fails to express: still, here is a conception which can be made to cover many of the truths that govern the interior life of prayer.

EVELYN UNDERHILL,
THE HOUSE OF THE SOUL

TEN
What's a Woman to Do?

𝒯he evening air was heavy as Bill and I left our bungalow to
drive up the hill to the hotel that housed the Campus Crusade for
Christ headquarters. The Arrowhead Springs property had a
unique quietness about it. As I enjoyed the beauty, I caught
myself listening for the joyful voices of the young people who
filled the grounds with energy.

Bill and I had spent the day working on projects, answering
phone calls, and meeting with people. It was dinnertime, and we
had been invited to join a group of more than two hundred
young people who were part of the STINT (Short-Term International) missions team. The group was composed of college
students who had committed one year of their lives to an international mission project. This particular group was going to Latin
America and to the Orient. They had spent several days preparing, including orientation of cultural aspects, language, team
building, and evangelism training.

As I stepped out of the car and heard voices coming from the
pool area, my mind flashed back to so many similar events and the
excitement of people preparing to serve the Lord Jesus. What a privi-

lege to take the message of the gospel to those who need to hear of God's love! We joined the group for dinner and shared from our hearts with them. Then we had a time of prayer and commissioning.

As I participated in the commissioning, I once again reaffirmed the truth that preparation for any area of service needs to be prayerfully and thoughtfully structured. We must equip ourselves with the knowledge of God's Word and the practical skills necessary to share our faith and serve others.

Acquiring knowledge and wisdom is a lifelong adventure for the Christian. New opportunities and challenges face us daily, and remaining informed and ready to serve requires careful attention. From the beginning our teams have been encouraged to acquire knowledge from the Scriptures and to gain skills in boldly approaching students without offense. Above all, we must be intimately aware of the Holy Spirit and trust God to meet our needs, recognizing that all God requires of us is our availability. He will do the rest.

That is what "Acquiring Our Skills" is about—learning how to walk with God and serve Him with the skills He builds into our lives. In the next few chapters we will discover how to find God's will, bear spiritual fruit, study the Bible and pray, serve others with the right attitude, and share our faith. Each of these is a skill that can be learned as we grow in the Spirit's control.

A Step of Faith

Although the headquarters of Campus Crusade for Christ in now located in Orlando, Florida, it was located for over thirty years in

Arrowhead Springs in the San Bernardino Mountains. Until our ministry outgrew the location, it was the hub of the worldwide center. Conferences, meetings, offices, prayer efforts, training, all were clustered in the beautiful foothills overlooking the city of San Bernardino. Bill and I lived in a bungalow on the grounds.

The way Arrowhead Springs became our international headquarters was a miracle of God. If Bill hadn't been so sure that God was leading us there, we would have missed the great opportunity He had for us.

The events unfolded in 1962. Our staff had grown to almost two hundred people, and we needed more room. We had long outgrown the house in Bel Air.

Bill brought me to Arrowhead Springs to consider purchasing the former luxury hotel, which had closed about four and a half years earlier. We looked at the 136-room hotel, the ten cottages, two large dormitories, and other buildings on 1,800 acres of land. Neither of us knew anything about operating a hotel or looking after the buildings and grounds. I thought the work would kill us.

As we stood in the beautiful Wahni Room of the hotel, overlooking the San Bernardino Valley, Bill said, "Honey, I have the assurance that God wants us to have Arrowhead Springs for this ministry. We'll be in place this fall!" Bill was certain that God intended Arrowhead Springs to be the headquarters for Campus Crusade and that the facility would accelerate our ministry growth beyond anything we could imagine.

Lacking his faith, I replied, "Dear, you must be crazy! Even if we were able to purchase Arrowhead Springs by fall, we wouldn't want to move in until it was adequately refurbished."

With us were a professional builder and his wife, an interior decorator. The woman turned to Bill and said lightly, "Bill, I'm going to pray for you."

He quickly replied, "Don't pray for me. Pray for my wife."

We did move into that building by fall. I was amazed to see how God miraculously provided the financing and the people with expertise to help operate Arrowhead Springs. Seeing Bill's faith in God's ability and leading helped expand my faith to trust God for whatever He wanted me to do. When God calls us to a task and we make ourselves available to Him, He gives us the ability to manage the circumstances, and He provides the finances to do whatever is necessary to accomplish the task.

Seeing Bill's faith in God's ability and leading helped expand my faith to trust God for whatever He wanted me to do.

In seeking God's will and acting according to His guidance, we can look for four voices that will help us discern His plan for our lives.

Four "Voices"

As believers who have chosen God's over-all plan for our lives, we find ourselves confronted with the problem of guidance in many situations: "Should I, or shouldn't I?" There are several ways, or "voices," God uses to help us find His will.

GOD'S LEADING WILL NEVER BE CONTRARY TO HIS WORD
God's Word is the final authority in all our decisions. For example, if you are tempted to take something that doesn't belong to you, you would not have to ask God if it were permissible to steal

because God's Word says clearly, "Do not steal" (Exodus 20:15). For the same reason, we should never ask God whether it is His will that we marry an unbeliever because His Word tells us, "Do not be yoked together with unbelievers" (2 Corinthians 6:14, NIV). Wherever God's Word gives commands and clear principles, they are not to be questioned because they are obviously God's will.

Scripture is also the guideline for less definitive choices. Anytime my husband and I had an important decision to make and the direction was not clear, we sought the answer from Scripture. At one time we wanted to have a third child. We mentioned this to some friends, and one day while Bill was on a trip, I received a telephone call that someone wished to place a baby girl in our home for adoption. Since we had two boys already, I thought this was an answer to prayer.

I could hardly wait to share the news with Bill when he arrived home. I knew he would be excited. But when I told him, he completely surprised me by not saying yes.

For hours we discussed the pros and cons of taking a new baby into our home. Because I was emotionally involved in the decision—I wanted to have a little girl—I was not fully considering the other option. But when we went to bed that night, I prayed that if God wanted us to adopt her, He would confirm it in my heart. If we were not to take this step, I asked to know from His Word that this was definitely not His plan for us.

The next day a staff member came to visit. She had just purchased the newly released Amplified version of the Old Testament and enthusiastically read Proverbs 31 to me. As I listened, verse 16 caught my attention: "She considers a new field before she buys or accepts it—expanding prudently [and not courting neglect of her present duties by assuming others]. With her savings [of time and strength] she plants fruitful vines in her vineyard."

Suddenly I realized that I had all I could handle with the family God had given me and with the increasing responsibilities of an expanding ministry. This verse confirmed to me the decision we should make, and at the same time, as I accepted God's will in this situation, He took away all my intense emotion of wanting a daughter.

MANY TIMES GOD'S LEADING IS MADE CLEAR BY CIRCUMSTANCES

Christians frequently have no problem discerning God's will because God opens one door and closes another. However, at other times He gives us opportunities to wait upon Him and seek His counsel as He leaves open two or more doors. This experience is quite common, especially for those who have walked with the Lord for some time.

If you encounter a situation with more than one choice and no immediate decision has to be made, I would encourage you to wait on God's leading. George Mueller, whose faith God so marvelously honored, said, "The Lord orders our stops as well as our steps." When the time comes that a decision must be made, you can proceed in the direction that seems best, making sure that all other "voices" about your choice agree.

Some Christians follow the practice of Gideon by putting out a "fleece"—asking God to show them the right choice by giving them a particular sign. But this will not automatically point to God's will. Remember, Gideon had no Bible or indwelling Holy

Spirit, and he lived during a time of great crisis. We find no similar instruction for us. In fact, Jesus tells us in Matthew 12:39, "Only an evil, faithless generation would ask for a miraculous sign." We are to walk by faith and not by sight, knowing that God desires having His way in our lives more than we do.

LISTEN TO YOUR INNER VOICE

Only since the Day of Pentecost have believers been permanently indwelt by the Spirit. Therefore, as Christians we are the first of God's people to have an inner voice. However, because our sin nature has a voice too, we can easily mistake the voice of the flesh for the inner urgings of the Spirit. We must always check our inner voice to make sure it's in harmony with God's Word.

When a person is under strong emotional influences, she is open to impressions that may be merely emotional rather than spiritual. During those times, she can easily believe that her emotional response is from the Lord. But nothing is more unreliable.

For example, a young couple agreed after prayer that they should pledge $100 toward a church building program. While attending a fund-raising meeting, the husband named the sum they had decided they should pledge. Because the amount of pledges was mounting slowly, an impassioned plea went out for members to give sacrificially. Suddenly, the wife rose and pledged another hundred. As she sat down, she said to her surprised husband, "I have faith for more, haven't you?"

Her leading was contrary to their agreement and to God's Word, which says that "the wife must respect her husband"

(Ephesians 5:33). She should have waited until they had time to discuss and pray about raising the amount of their pledge.

Satan is the author of confusion and often appears as an angel of light to give a mistaken impression of duty. When he is leading, you will find yourself pulled first in one direction and then in another. At such a time, resist Satan and ask the Spirit to take control. Wait quietly before the Lord. Let Him speak to you: "This is the way; turn around and walk here" (Isaiah 30:21). When the Holy Spirit is guiding, you will experience quietness and peace within.

GOD EXPECTS US TO USE GOOD COMMON SENSE

Hannah Whitall Smith, author of *The Christian's Secret of a Happy Life*, remarked that doing the commonplace was a better foundation for doing good work for the Lord than any great ecstasies of inspiration. She said she had no consciousness that God was inspiring her to write a book that would bless millions of hearts. She was merely helping her husband by writing a series of articles for his magazine. Those articles proved so popular and helpful that they appeared in book form. God simply used her availability.

Part of using our good common sense is listening to the advice of other growing Christians. Proverbs 15:22 says, "Plans fail for lack of counsel, but with many advisers they succeed" (NIV). I have seen many occasions where believers think God is leading them in a certain direction, so they refuse to weigh counsel from godly friends. Then they make a huge mistake. Sometimes when we are emotionally involved in a choice, we need to seek the advice of more objective people. God won't always lead us according to the advice others give us, but He does ask us to prayerfully consider what our friends have to say.

Sometimes occasions arise that require immediate decisions, and we have no time to ponder the matter. Aware of our own insufficiency and trusting in God for everything, we must proceed with the confidence that He is directing our paths. We are promised, "He leads the humble in what is right, teaching them his way" (Psalm 25:9). When we walk in the Spirit, He will guide us to the right choices.

In seeking God's will, we should look for the four voices to be in agreement: the Scriptures, the indwelling Spirit, circumstances, and good common sense. They will all testify that this is God's way.

When We Have No Control

What about situations over which we have no control? Can we find God's leading then?

In the face of trouble, the world consoles itself with pious platitudes, such as "every cloud has a silver lining," or adopts a fatalistic attitude: "whatever will be will be." In many cases, unbelievers bravely take calamities "on the chin" and live with the results.

How we meet seeming disaster, loss, trials, and bereavement will prove whether we trust God. No matter how little we can change about our circumstances, we always have a choice about our attitude toward the situation.

When faced with adversity, the Christian woman comforts herself with the knowledge that all of life's events are in the hands of God. This is the secret of triumphantly meeting the sorrows that come to us: "They [the righteous] do not fear bad news; they confidently trust the Lord to care for them" (Psalm 112:7).

A great Bible expositor, while speaking at a convention, stated that for some time he had been pondering the reason for that threefold description of God's will as good, acceptable, and perfect as given in Romans 12:2. He felt he had received new light on it as he contemplated those words in relation to the three sayings of the Lord Jesus in the garden of Gethsemane as He struggled with the burden of doing God's will by dying for us. The expositor was well aware that the Lord's cup of suffering could not compare with ours, yet the Lord's attitude of submission to His Father's will can be an example as we meet the trying circumstances of life.

When faced with adversity, the Christian woman comforts herself with the knowledge that all of life's events are in the hands of God.

GOD'S WILL IS GOOD

Most Christians will agree that God's will is best for them. But when faced with some threatened calamity, their hearts cry out to God, as Jesus did: "If it is possible, let this cup of suffering be taken away from me" (Matthew 26:39). There is nothing wrong with that prayer, but if it is not answered the way you want it to be, what then? Will you still see God's will as good, as Jesus did?

GOD'S WILL IS ACCEPTABLE

Our Lord went a step further. He prayed again in Matthew 26:42, "My Father! If this cup cannot be taken away until I drink it, your will be done." We find no mention of His own will or desires here. He accepts the Father's will.

What God has ordered in the life of the believer must be accepted. Job was one of the world's greatest examples of suffering and affliction. When God allowed Satan to put his hand on all that Job had, Job said, "The Lord gave me everything I had, and the Lord has taken it away. Praise the name of the Lord!" (Job 1:21). Again, in reply to his three friends who came to mourn with him and comfort him, Job expressed his trust in God, "Though he slay me, yet will I hope in him" (Job 13:15, NIV).

This is the faith that Paul voiced in Romans 8:28: "We know that in all things God works for the good of those who love him, who have been called according to his purpose" (NIV). Do we find God's will acceptable? No matter what God allows to come into our lives, we accept it as His will and handle it through His Spirit with a godly attitude.

GOD'S WILL IS PERFECT

We can become so engrossed in a trial or tragedy that we do not see beyond it. We must not stop short of the final stage—seeing God's will as perfect no matter how difficult it may be. This is Jesus' attitude when He said, "Shall I not drink from the cup the Father has given me?" (John 18:11).

What words of triumph! The Father placed into the hand of His dearly beloved Son a cup that was bitter, full to the brim with the world's sin and woe. The cup represents the sufferings of the

Lord, the cross, and the shame. Jesus joyfully received it because it was the loving Father who gave it to Him. This was not resignation; this was not just submission; it was joyful acceptance.

Psalm 40:8 says, "I take joy in doing your will, my God." Will you accept the cup that the Father puts to your lips and cry in triumph, "Shall I not drink from this cup?" You must look beyond the trial and the disaster, holding on to the fact there is a blessing in that cup. The Father knows the mixture that will work for your highest good.

Can you make this your prayer? "Lord, make me radiantly triumphant." Although your heart may be breaking and your eyes filled with tears, the indwelling Spirit will enable you to take the cup and receive it as God's good, acceptable, and perfect will for you. And as He comforts you, He will use you to comfort others with the comfort He has given to you (2 Corinthians 1:4).

From the Hand of God

One truth you can be sure of: God's will for you is better than any other pathway in life. No matter how difficult, how lonely, or how uncomfortable, following God's guidance will lead to joy, peace, and contentment. It is the salve that soothes the insecurities of our inner woman.

You will be amazed at how creative God will be in directing your life. His plan for you is different from His plan for any other person in history. He deals with us as His unique creatures, formed by His hand, developed by His Spirit, and led by His voice.

Let me show you a contrast in how God leads His children. A young missionary answered God's call to go to Japan and teach in a mission school. While on furlough, she learned that her aged mother and invalid sister were in great need physically and financially. She had responded to God's call to "go into all the world and preach the gospel," but now her sense of duty told her that she must remain and care for them. The voice telling her to return to Japan would not have harmonized with 1 Timothy 5:8: "Those who won't care for their own relatives, especially those living in the same household, have denied what we believe. Such people are worse than unbelievers." So she did not return to her mission school. Her sacrifice to remain at home far exceeded the one she had made when she left friends and loved ones for foreign shores.

God in His goodness, however, changed the locale of her ministry. He continued to use her mightily as she taught in a Bible college and inspired others to go in her place. God's plans for her were perfect.

Now let me tell you the story of another woman. In 1930 Gladys Aylward applied to be a missionary with the China Inland Mission, but she was turned down because of her poor academic abilities. She was so sure that God wanted her to serve Him in China that she began saving her pennies, determined to go on her own. She diligently studied the Chinese language and customs. Then she bought a railway ticket through Europe, Russia, and Siberia, and into China. At the time she traveled, Russia was involved in a war with China, so Gladys shared space in trains packed with soldiers. Only by the grace of God was she able to arrive at her destination in Manchuria.

Then Gladys had to trek across the mountains to Yangchen. There she worked with another single missionary, who soon died. In a time of hardship for Gladys, the Chinese government hired her as a foot inspector. (The government had decreed female foot binding to be illegal.) She could freely go into homes and talk to many women.

God kept leading Gladys through hardships and exciting ministry until she retired in 1957. A biography of her life *(The Small Woman)* and a film *(The Inn of the Sixth Happiness)* spread her story throughout the world. She even met with Queen Elizabeth.

Which woman served God most faithfully? Both! They were available and willing to serve to the end.

Gladys Aylward lived in a time when women normally didn't serve alone on the front line of missions. This is what she said at the end of her life: "I wasn't God's first choice for what I've done for China. There was somebody else. . . . I don't know who it was—God's first choice. It must have been a man—a wonderful man. A well-educated man. I don't know what happened. Perhaps he died. Perhaps he wasn't willing. . . . And God looked down . . . and saw Gladys Aylward."[1]

That's my desire in doing God's will—that He looks down and sees Vonette Bright, willing, available, and anxious to do His will. That's all God requires—not that we're smart, talented, rich, chic, or any other quality; only that we follow His guidance and are content in the center of His will, during hard times and times of blessing.

Is that your desire too? If it is, I can attest that it is the most glorious way to live!

ELEVEN

Clear Evidence

The apostle Paul writes: "Keep putting into practice all you learned from me and heard from me and saw me doing, and the God of peace will be with you" (Philippians 4:9). When Paul wrote this, the believers in Philippi were facing many of the problems that confront us today—an immoral society, an unpopular message, a sometimes-hostile government. But because Paul devoted his every breath to following the Lord, he knew he could challenge others to follow Him.

I watched my dear friend Dr. Henrietta Mears display a similar confidence. As the director of Christian Education at First Presbyterian Church of Hollywood, she had been very influential in helping to teach my husband about the Christian life.

Physically, Henrietta Mears wasn't the most beautiful person I've ever met. She was large boned and stocky and her dramatic features were accentuated by thick-lensed glasses. Yet, if anyone should ask me, "Who is the most beautiful person you have ever known?" Henrietta Mears would be at the top of my list. Miss Mears had an inner quality that caused all who knew her to see beyond her appearance. She had a vibrant personality and was adamant that knowing Christ was the most exciting adventure a person could ever experience.

While sharing a home in Bel Air with Miss Mears for ten years, I learned that love was the quality she longed for most in her life. All who knew her would probably agree that she was the most loving person they'd ever known. However, as she often stated, she hadn't always been that way, but God was continually building that quality into her. As Miss Mears expressed her love to others, she encouraged all who knew her to strive for, and usually to attain, the highest achievement she thought possible of them. Her example and her teaching produced much fruit. As a result of her encouragement, we know of more than four hundred men who served in pulpits and many men and women who served on mission fields, in business, and in other professions as God's ambassadors. There is no way to know how many families established godly homes as a result of her teaching.

Miss Mears had inner beauty because the love of God shone through her life. She readily confessed that she was the person she was because Jesus Christ had changed her.

That same radiant, fruitful lifestyle is available to every Christian, and it is the most exciting and attractive one possible. It causes people to take notice. This radiance, which cannot be hidden, can be ours as we seek to trust and obey the Lord. It is a goal worth striving for. As Miss Mears would say, "Who would want anything but the best?"

Bearing Fruit in Bel Air

Bearing fruit—both in the qualities we display in our lives and in the people we influence for Christ—is the responsibility of every

Christian. Our Lord has planted us here to bring forth fruit. He said to His disciples, "My true disciples produce much fruit. This brings great glory to my Father" (John 15:8). Just as He looked for fruit in their lives, He comes seeking fruit in every believer's life, for it is in the fruit that the Father is glorified.

I had a period in my life when I overlooked fruit bearing. You remember the story I told about the time I felt like a martyr when I was living in Bel Air, had a baby to care for, and was trying to help Bill with the ministry to college students. I had already surrendered my life to God by signing the contract, but I still suffered from a rebellious and ungrateful spirit in this area. My circumstances had revealed this hard place in my heart.

At the time, I was excited about receiving Christ: I knew that my prayers were now heard, and I experienced answers. My life began to take a new direction. Areas of my life that I had tried to improve now seemed under control. I knew my sins were forgiven, I had eternal life, and I had the promise from Jesus that my life would be full and meaningful. However, when I found myself in a huge house with my routine, boring, domestic chores, it hardly seemed that I was bearing fruit. At times I asked myself, "Where is the reality of being a Christian in this situation?"

I may have been living in Bel Air, but I had never felt so abused before. It seemed people were taking advantage of me and expecting more than I was physically capable of doing. I was also resentful because I knew I could accomplish more significant tasks and participate in more glamorous activities than being a housekeeper. That did not seem to be a fruit-bearing activity.

What I found was that I could not change my attitude on my own. When I tried, I just grew more resentful. But I could renew my surrender to God, who could change my attitude! Desperately I prayed that God would give me an answer. First, I decided to ask God to take us out of that huge house. But when no one else was excited about the idea, I realized God was going to leave me there to teach me something—even though I wasn't sure I wanted to learn it.

A few days later, alone in the quiet of our bedroom, I knelt at the window seat in prayer and submitted my will to Him. My prayer was, "Lord, if You're going to leave me here in this house with these circumstances, You will have to make me willing to be made willing to learn what You want me to learn."

I became aware of one very important concept I had missed before: my attitude—not my circumstances— was what was making me unhappy.

That prayer changed the course of my life. I became aware of one very important concept I had missed before: my attitude—not my circumstances—was what was making me unhappy. At last I was willing to learn the things God wanted to teach me.

You would not believe what happened! He helped me organize that home in the most amazing manner, and I could not have been happier. After a few weeks the house was running like clockwork. I found I could do more than one task at a time. By changing my negative attitude, I discovered creative energy I had not known I had. I truly began to enjoy my home, to accept it as my ministry, and I was challenged to reach my greatest personal potential right where God had placed me.

Then, when I had learned the lesson He wanted me to learn,

along came someone to help with my work. God sent enough domestic help to relieve me of some of the responsibility. Also, when students came for counseling, they would often say, "Isn't there something I can do to help?" I found I could mend clothes or sew on buttons, and they could iron handkerchiefs or table-cloths while I counseled with them. When I was preparing dinner, I would invite them into the kitchen and continue to cook my meals as I was counseling. By allowing them to help, they felt like a greater part of my life. Talking and sharing with each other was even more meaningful as we worked together.

Now I went about with a song in my heart, realizing this was what God wanted me to do. If this was the way in which I could please Him most, this was what I wanted to do. I was beginning to learn how God produces the fruit of the Spirit in my life.

I am confident that had I not learned this lesson early in our ministry, I would have struggled with my attitude to this day and missed out on some of the dearest blessings that come with having a servant attitude.

The Vine and the Branches

If you travel through wine country after pruning season, you will see acres of stark fruit canes. They look gnarled and dead—but they aren't. Inside the woody stalk runs the sap that will eventu-ally produce tendrils, vines, flowers, and finally fruit. Then, come summer when the fruit is fully ripened, the grapes have a sweet pulp that drips with delicious juice.

When you look at those pruned stalks, you see no outward

beauty. It's inside where the sap runs that the beauty lies. That truth applies to our woman within. Our inner beauty is what counts, and we have a radiance as we walk and talk with God.

Training is necessary to develop a fruitful grapevine. Often the only way to regulate the crop is to prune the young vine. Pruning determines not only the quality of fruit but also the quality of the wood for the next year's growth. During the annual pruning, 90 to 95 percent of the year's growth is removed.

Jesus taught that we are like branches and He is the vine: "I am the true vine, and my Father is the gardener" (John 15:1). Jesus says in verse 4, "Remain in me, and I will remain in you. For a branch cannot produce fruit if it is severed from the vine, and you cannot be fruitful apart from me."

What does it mean to remain in Jesus? The grapevine gives us the answer. As long as the branch remains connected to the vine, sap runs from the vine into the branch, and the branch can bear fruit. But if the branch is separated from the vine, not only is there no fruit but the life in the branch withers. The branch becomes worthless.

Norman B. Harrison says, "Abiding is the key to Christian experience by which the divine attributes are transplanted into human soil, to the transforming of character and conduct."

When I became dissatisfied with my situation in the Bel Air home, I was not abiding in Christ. I was letting my circumstances dictate my behavior and attitude. I have learned that when I look at my circumstances, it is easy to become discouraged and defeated, and that's when I am not making myself available to God.

Scripture tells us the solution for this problem: "Let heaven fill your thoughts. Do not think only about things down here on earth. For you died when Christ died, and your real life is hidden with Christ in God" (Colossians 3:2-3). I am to look to Christ in every situation—to set my sights and affection on Him—and then I will have victory. That's exactly what I did when I prayed and turned the situation over to God's control. That allowed the "sap to run" through me. As I allowed myself to be used by God, Christ's Holy Spirit living in me changed my attitude and actions.

As we abide in Christ, we will be obedient to His Word and will experience the Father's love. (Read John 15:9-11.) The result of abiding in Christ is the abundant joy that He produces in our lives.

Abiding in Christ will inevitably cause us to love others as Christ loves us. You can be sure that you are abiding in Christ if you are able to have a Christlike love toward the people who irritate you most. When we do this, we become friends of God.

It is not only a privilege to abide in Christ; it is also a command. As God's friends, we are commanded: "You did not choose me, but I chose you and appointed you to go and bear fruit—fruit that will last" (John 15:16, NIV).

> *You can be sure that you are abiding in Christ if you are able to have a Christlike love toward the people who irritate you most.*

What Is Fruit?

The question often arises, then, What does Jesus mean by fruit? What am I supposed to bear when I abide in Him?

One form of fruit is bringing others to Jesus. In Matthew

4:18-20, Peter and Andrew were fishing in the Sea of Galilee. They were minding their own business, caught up in the necessity of providing for themselves. Then Jesus came along and called to them, "Come, be my disciples, and I will show you how to fish for people!" Peter and Andrew immediately left all they owned and followed Jesus.

What was Jesus asking them to do? In "fishing for people," they would be telling the good news of salvation to others and bringing them to Jesus. That is bearing fruit in God's kingdom.

A second form of fruit is the fruit of the Spirit. Galatians 5:22 tells us, "When the Holy Spirit controls our lives, he will produce this kind of fruit in us: love, joy, peace, patience, kindness, goodness, faithfulness, gentleness, and self-control." These point back to the attitudes that we have when we are filled with (controlled by) the Holy Spirit.

When I turned my situation over to God that day, He produced both kinds of fruit in my life. I was more patient in the work He had given me, and I fulfilled my responsibilities more faithfully. At the same time, I was bearing fruit by counseling young women and telling them about the Savior.

These two kinds of fruit are intertwined. I cannot lead people to Christ if I display bad attitudes. On the other hand, when my attitudes are Spirit led, I will desire to share my faith with everyone I meet.

The Pruning Process

The passage in John 15 also describes another essential element in bearing fruit—pruning. "He cuts off every branch that doesn't produce fruit, and he prunes the branches that do bear fruit so they will produce even more" (John 15:2). What does it mean that Jesus prunes the branches?

Think back to the last time you grew significantly in your faith. Was it when times were good? Or was it during a trial that kept you dependent on God for help?

We can learn about God during good circumstances, but many times God uses difficult circumstances to teach us and to prune away the unfruitful branches in our lives. And that can be painful for the moment.

A pastor once asked his congregation, "Is there someone at your workplace who irritates you? Have you asked God to relieve you of the burden of this person and He didn't reply? God is allowing that person to be in your life as holy sandpaper to smooth off your rough edges. He won't remove the irritation until you have learned the lesson that He wants to teach you."

In Bel Air the Lord was pruning me because He could see that my attitude needed an adjustment. He knew I felt that I deserved better treatment than what I was receiving. Instead, I should have had my eye on the prize of winning students to Christ—no matter what I had to do to accomplish that goal. God knew that my wrong attitude would hinder my future involvement in the ministry. He was pruning me so that I could bear fruit for many years.

What does God need to prune in your life? Are you producing both kinds of fruit? Which fruit of the Spirit is lacking when you're in difficult situations? Do you have trouble witnessing to friends and family members?

Abiding in Christ enables us to live victorious, fruitful lives.

We will never convince anyone that we truly love the Lord unless we obey Him, and this includes bearing fruit for Him. The only way we can demonstrate that we are abiding in Him is to love people with patience, gentleness, faithfulness, and the other fruits of the Spirit, thereby introducing them to our Savior.

TWELVE

Feeding My Mind

$\mathcal{E}$very day of my life as the wife of Bill Bright was an adventure. New challenges to face, new opportunities for ministry, new people to meet, and interesting places to visit filled me with daily anticipation to see what God would allow us to do. Through all the excitement and adventure, my relationship with my husband was a priority. I could not let all the wonderful events in our life crowd out the most precious relationship God entrusted to me in the person of my husband.

That is also true of my spiritual life. Christianity is a living relationship with the person of Jesus Christ. However, as with any meaningful relationship, we must work at it. If I hadn't made Christ the priority in my life, other things would have crowded between us. Good things like raising children, entertaining guests, and traveling for the ministry can take the place of my time with God. Just as we are available to talk with, listen to, and do things for those we love, so we must spend time in the same manner getting to know Jesus Christ.

Once we experience spiritual birth, we must have spiritual nourishment to grow. The only source of information about

Christ is the Bible. To deepen my relationship with Jesus, I have to study Scripture to know what it says about Him and His kingdom.

Just as a newborn is initially fed milk and later moves on to juices and then eventually soft foods, so it should be with us as spiritual infants. When we first become Christians, we should begin to study His Word and act upon what we know. Just as babies are not concerned with what they can't eat but concentrate on what they can, so should new Christians concentrate on what they can understand in the Word of God.

Tragically, many people who have been Christians long enough to be quite mature in their spiritual walk remain spiritual babies. A woman who does not spend time alone with the Lord and with His Word limits herself. She cannot know the rewards of a spiritually productive or abundant life as well as the person who daily searches the Scriptures.

I have known individuals who received Christ and began their spiritual walk on the same day because they immediately got into the Word of God. As they began to apply spiritual truths to their lives, they really "took off" as Christians. Others were slow to grow because they gave Bible study a low priority in their lives and consequently did not learn how to apply spiritual truths.

If you have raised teenagers, you can recall how those years were questioning ones in which your children were trying to establish their own spiritual foundations. When Zac was in high school, occasionally he came home from school and said, "Mother, how do you really know the Christian position is right?"

I gave him many answers, but one point made a lasting impression when others didn't have much impact. I would say, "Look at the lifestyle of the true follower of Christ. Isn't it attractive? Now think about the lifestyle of the non-Christian. Do you find many appealing qualities?"

Zac would then come to the conclusion that the imitation of the life of Christ was the most exciting way to live. To imitate Christ, we must learn more about Him and His way of life. That's an essential purpose for Bible study.

The King's Story

The Old Testament gives us the story of one king of Israel who was deeply impacted by the Word of God. Josiah was born during a time when the nation of Israel had forsaken God to follow after idolatry. The morals of the people plummeted. In fact, things were so bad that his father, King Amon, was murdered by his own officials, which meant that eight-year-old Josiah was crowned king.

After Josiah became king, he wanted to know about Jehovah, the God of his ancestor David. At age twenty Josiah began to tear down all the pagan temples and six years later to rebuild the Temple of the Lord, which was in terrible disrepair. For a young man, he certainly had a heart for God. Yet there was still something missing. The people didn't have the Word of God to read, just biblical knowledge passed down from one generation to another.

During the Temple reconstruction, the "Book of the Law of

the Lord" was discovered and taken to Josiah. What was Josiah's reaction when he heard the Word of God read before him? He tore his robes, realizing how far he and his people had strayed from God's holy standard. He began to understand that God's judgment would be upon His people because they had disobeyed and dishonored Him by worshiping idols.

He immediately sent his officials to consult the prophetess of God, Huldah, about what to do to turn away God's wrath. Huldah told them that God had seen the king's sorrow and repentance, and God was pleased.

When the men reported back to him, the king assembled all the people and had the Book of the Law read aloud to them. He then publicly renewed his commitment to follow the Lord and to obey all that was in God's Word. The people, who saw his example and devotion, also pledged themselves to obey God.

The rest of his life, Josiah stayed true to God. He diligently followed all the commands in God's Law.

The Bible Is Our Lifeline

Just as King Josiah believed, Scripture is relevant to every phase of our lives. It is our lifeline. I believe that one of the great needs of this day is for us to know what the Bible has to say and to act upon that knowledge. Today, when no authority seems to rule our conduct, we need to return to God's textbook for man.

As we read the Bible, we find explicit direction in personal matters that concern us. For example, we learn how to be a loving husband, how to be a respectful wife, how to discipline and raise children, how to handle our relationships with other people. God's Word speaks explicitly about topics ranging from court decisions to moral conduct.

For example, a friend of mine who operated her own business was sued. Her lawyer assured her that the individual who brought the suit didn't have a case, yet my friend lost. After the trial, one of the jurors came up to her to apologize that the decision had to be made against her. The juror said, "We knew you weren't guilty, but we also knew that you could afford to pay this penalty. Since there was financial need on the part of the other person, we decided in his favor."

In Exodus 23:3 we have clear instruction: "Do not slant your testimony in favor of a person just because that person is poor." This would, of course, apply to the rich man as well. In executing justice, an understanding of the Word of God would have led the jurors to render a different decision.

A schoolteacher tells of a problem she faced in her classroom. A little boy had lost twenty-five cents and was quite distressed. Trying to comfort him, she instructed the class to look for the quarter. After the children had been looking for a while, she thought, *Surely someone should have found it by now.* When she asked the class, one little boy spoke up and said he had found the quarter.

"You need to return it," the teacher suggested.

The boy replied, "I will not. He lost it, and I found it. So the quarter is mine."

Nothing she said would convince the young man to give the quarter back to the boy who had lost it. The teacher left the classroom bewildered about what to do. Obviously, the value system of the class was, "Finders keepers. Tough luck for the guy who loses it."

In the Bible we see a different set of values. We are told that if we find something that was lost, we are to return it to the owner, even if the owner is our "enemy" (Exodus 23:4).

If we neglect the Bible, we cannot expect to benefit from the wisdom and direction that result from knowing God's Word.

If we neglect the Bible, we cannot expect to benefit from the wisdom and direction that result from knowing God's Word. Only as we learn Scripture can we apply it to our lives, and learning takes time and effort. Hebrews 4:12 tells us, "The word of God is living and active. Sharper than any double-edged sword, it penetrates even to dividing soul and spirit, joints and marrow; it judges the thoughts and attitudes of the heart" (NIV). God's Word strengthens us, bringing peace to our hearts and direction to our lives. Decisions that are made in light of God's Word show wisdom.

Finding the Time

To get to know God and make His Word an integral part of your life, use three different methods of learning the Bible: studying, reading, and memorizing. Each is important to your spiritual growth.

Studying helps you look deeply into what God has to say to you. If you find that studying the Bible is uninteresting or that it is difficult to make time for it, I understand. As a new Christian I had to concentrate on finding time to read my Bible and then discipline myself to apply the principle. But studying God's Word is essential to our spiritual health. You can find many Bible study helps in your local Christian bookstore, but be sure to make the Bible the main focus of your study rather than extra materials.

To learn more about the Bible, you may want to attend a Bible study group. There is something so special about sharing your experiences in the Word with other women who love God. I encourage you to form your own Sister Circle to study weekly or monthly with others. Nothing, however, can take the place of your personal study. You need time alone to communicate with God. Try to spend time daily with the Lord, even if it's just five to fifteen minutes.

Reading the Scriptures is also a necessity for me because I can't function well without a prolonged time of Bible reading. When my children were small, reading even a verse or two would sustain me through times of weariness. But today, with the special pressures of decisions and administrative responsibilities, that time in God's Word is vital for sensing His direction and guidance.

Reading the Bible, with its histories, genealogies, and strange names, can be an overwhelming experience for many. Let me give you some suggestions on how to begin. The Gospel of John is a good place to start your reading. I have found it helpful to underline all the verses that admonish us to believe and emphasize what we are to believe.

After reading the Gospel of John, you may wish to go on to Acts and Romans. Acts is a particularly important book because it tells the story of the early church, its leaders, and God's miracles. The book of Romans explains what man is like without God, his need for a Savior, why it was necessary that Jesus Christ came, and the difference between a life governed by self and a life governed by the Holy Spirit.

Next, read the New Testament through as quickly as possible. It can be completed in about twenty-five hours. Read it two or three times before you go on to the Old Testament, then read the Old Testament as quickly as possible.

As you mature in your walk, you will want to spend an hour or more reading and studying God's Word each day.

Also, memorize verses that are important to you. As I have said before, Bill and I were committed to making all our decisions based on God's Word because we knew that we are human and can fail to understand God's will for our lives. We memorized His Word so that when a decision came up unexpectedly and we didn't have an opportunity to search the Scriptures, the Holy Spirit could remind us of a verse that applied to our situation. Sometimes, memorized verses comforted us in the swirl of a crisis. We meditated on God's Word when we had a few moments driving in the car or sitting in a doctor's office.

I am only one person, but as I have determined to apply scriptural principles to my life and have shared my knowledge with others, my life has influenced many for Jesus. You are only one, but as you make the same decision, it is possible for you to impact your world.

THIRTEEN

Conversations That Count

$\mathcal{H}$ow I thank God that He impressed upon Bill and me and our staff the importance of prayer when our ministry was first organized. I can't imagine where we would be today if we hadn't established a priority of prayer.

The first year that Bill and I lived near the UCLA campus, we organized a continuous prayer chain by dividing twenty-four hours into 96 fifteen-minute periods. Volunteers from all over the country signed up to pray during a particular fifteen-minute time slot. That year we saw 250 students respond to the gospel of Jesus Christ!

Later, as the ministry grew, we began to have a great concern for our nation, which led to a united prayer effort called the Great Commission Prayer Crusade. This ministry, which I had the privilege of directing, was born to give women throughout the nation a united opportunity to influence its moral and spiritual values.

As I look back on the ministry of the Great Commission Prayer Crusade, we saw amazing answers to prayer. In one city a teenage girl was kidnapped. What agony that caused! After three long weeks of searching, many people gave her up for dead. But others were still united in prayer in that city, and she was returned unharmed and unmolested!

When the Vietnam War ended, thousands of refugees fled to South Vietnam. They were housed in refugee camps until sponsors were found to help them settle in a new homeland. Thousands of Christians prayed for the physical and spiritual needs of the refugees. In December 1975 the last of the refugee camps was closed because the remaining refugees had located sponsors. Of the 131,000 displaced Vietnamese people, more than 80,000 found sponsors through church-related groups!

I learned that God is both intimate and universal. Nothing is too small or too large for Him to handle.

As you can see, our prayer efforts covered larger issues as well as those of a personal nature. Through this I learned that God is both intimate and universal. Nothing is too small or too large for Him to handle. Today, in my personal life as well as in the ministry of Campus Crusade, prayer is top priority.

The Importance of Prayer

Tragically, Christians are often misinformed about the role of prayer. God speaks to us through His Word, but to cultivate this relationship, we communicate with God through prayer. Unfortunately, the prayers of countless people never go beyond "now I lay me down to sleep" or "God bless the missionaries." Many pray only in emergencies or find prayer so boring that they don't pray at all. Some neglect prayer because they don't feel worthy enough to approach God. Have you ever found yourself in one of these categories?

Prayer is so important that Jesus found it necessary to pray often, and by His words and His example He taught His disciples to pray. Throughout history the men and women through whom God accomplished much have relied on prayer for wisdom and power.

The following are some of the Bible's principles on the importance of prayer in our lives:

- We are to pray without ceasing (1 Thessalonians 5:17). We can talk to God hundreds of times throughout our day. No matter is too insignificant to bring to His attention or too difficult for His power.
- God will show us remarkable secrets when we call on Him (Jeremiah 33:3). He will reveal mysteries to us that we did not know.
- We don't have because we don't ask (James 4:2). God is waiting to answer our prayers, but we fail to acknowledge that we need His help, so we suffer the consequences.
- We will experience abundant joy through prayer (John 16:24). If you have ever seen God answer your desperate plea in His miraculous ways, you know what this verse is promising.

Prerequisites to Prayer

Jesus taught His disciples how to pray because we must come before God in a proper way. If we don't, our prayers will not be heard. The prerequisites God demands are necessary to enable us to have the deepest, most fruitful communion with our heavenly Father. The following are some of the most important prerequisites:

WE MUST BE RIGHTLY RELATED TO GOD

This means that we must be His children, born again into His family. For example, if a neighbor's little boy came up to me and asked, "Will you give me five dollars?" I might give him the money depending on the circumstances, but I am under no obligation to do so.

But if one of my sons came up to me and said, "Mommy, I need five dollars," I'd find out why he needed the money. If he answered, "I need to buy some material to do a science experiment," I'm obligated as his parent to provide for that need. Even if his reason is to buy a toy he's wanted for some time, I'd probably give it to him. The only time I would deny him is if my giving would harm him or the family.

With the first child, I had a choice. With my own son, my duty is to see to his needs. Also, because I love him, I try to give him what's in his best interest. And I receive great joy in giving to him.

That's similar to our relationship with God. Since I am His child, my heavenly Father evaluates my requests and provides for my needs. But the person who has not received Christ as her Savior has no guarantee that God will answer her request.

WE MUST HAVE A CLEAN HEART

In Psalm 66:18-20 the psalmist writes, "If I had not confessed the sin in my heart, my Lord would not have listened. But God did listen!

He paid attention to my prayer. Praise God, who did not ignore my prayer and did not withdraw his unfailing love from me."

This is another reason why we must keep short sin accounts with God. Just as a rebellious attitude in a child's heart will hinder his communication with his mother and father, our sin blocks the "telephone line" to heaven.

WE MUST HAVE A FORGIVING HEART

Jesus taught, "When you are praying, first forgive anyone you are holding a grudge against, so that your Father in heaven will forgive your sins, too" (Mark 11:25). An unforgiving attitude tempts us all at one time or another. Have you ever thought, *That person has hurt me so deeply that I can never forgive her?* God expects us to forgive others as He has forgiven us; we are to follow His example by having a forgiving heart. This verse doesn't refer to the one-time eternal forgiveness we receive at our spiritual birth. That has been secured through the sacrifice of Christ's blood. But it means that our communication with God will be interrupted because we are harboring a sin that is in direct opposition to God's forgiving nature.

> *God expects us to forgive others as He has forgiven us; we are to follow His example by having a forgiving heart.*

WE MUST PRAY IN JESUS' NAME

What Christ has done for us is so important because it provides the only way for us to approach God. When Jesus prepared His disciples for His return to heaven, He said, "At that time you won't need to ask me for anything. The truth is, you can go directly to the Father and ask him, and he will grant your request because you use my name" (John 16:23). It is only when we come before the Father in Jesus' name—which represents all that He is—that the Father hears and grants our requests.

WE MUST HAVE FAITH IN GOD'S ABILITY TO ANSWER OUR PRAYERS
Everything we do in the Christian life depends on faith. We were born again by faith. We walk in the Spirit by faith. Believing is a prerequisite for answered prayer (James 1:6-8).

Key Words for Prayer

Jesus gives us key concepts to guide our prayers. In John 15:7 Jesus tells us, "If you stay joined to me and my words remain in you, you may ask any request you like, and it will be granted!" I call this verse the combination to unlocking the "prayer safe" in heaven.

Imagine a bank vault with a gigantic door and a combination lock on the front. This safe contains the treasures of heaven. To open the door, you must apply the combination.

First, you turn the dial to the right until the line rests on "if you stay joined to me." The wheels inside the lock click; the first step is in place. This section of the verse is, of course, the concept of abiding in Christ. Since we can do nothing on our own but only in God's power, we must abide in Christ to have an effective prayer life.

Next, we turn the dial to the left until the line rests on "my words remain in you." The wheels click. God's Word is to be the guidebook for our requests. If what we want does not measure up to God's standards, we will not ask Him for it. If our request is in line with His Word, we can be assured that He will listen and answer.

Next, we turn the dial to the right until the marker lands on "ask any request you like." Because your will is lined up with God's will and your desires are consistent with His Word, your requests will please God. Click. The wheels snap into place once more.

Last, slide the dial left once more until the line lands on "it will be granted!" Now grab the giant vault door handle and pull. The door slides open effortlessly, and inside you see all the good things God intends for you!

Accepting God's Answer

As we abide in Christ, we will be able to accept God's answer—even when we find it difficult. Joni Eareckson Tada is an example of someone who has placed her complete trust in God and accepts His will for her life. Paralyzed at age nineteen in a diving accident, she struggled with understanding how God could allow this to happen to her. She desperately wanted to be healed. In her book *Secret Strength,* she describes her effort to understand why God wasn't answering her prayer like she wanted Him to:

> When I was first paralyzed, you can imagine how interested
> I was in what the Bible had to say about healing. I desperately
> wanted out of my wheelchair!

As I pored over Scripture, I was impressed with the kind of healing that Jesus performed. He never seemed to pass up anybody. He showed His concern for the suffering by opening the eyes of the blind and ears of the deaf—and even raising up the paralyzed.

I was also struck with the number of Bible verses that seemed to indicate I could ask whatever would be in God's will—and Jesus would do it. I put two and two together and figured if Jesus healed back then, He'd want to raise me up now. Why shouldn't He? Why shouldn't healing a suffering teenaged girl be perfectly consistent with His will?[1]

But Joni didn't experience healing. Instead, she continued to be afflicted by a body that limited her in almost every way. She couldn't use her hands or legs. She had to have help with all the intimate details of life. She tried so hard to understand what God means when He asks us to "pray in Jesus' name" and He will answer. Hadn't she done that?

Years later she began to comprehend God's plan. He wants us to pray for whatever is consistent with Christ's character because we are to be like Him. This is how she explains what she learned:

Jesus was a man of sorrows and acquainted with grief . . . yet there was a time when I thought words like suffering and disappointment shouldn't even be in the Christian's vocabulary.

Do you see what I'm saying? When we pray in Jesus' name, we should expect to receive qualities consistent with that name—with His character. Traits such as patience and self-control and assurance. We might pray for financial prosperity, a new career, success with the opposite sex, or physical healing, but God may choose to give us something even more precious, something even closer to what His name and character are all about.

His presence. His perspective. His endurance. His deep and lingering peace in the midst of turmoil and pain and loneliness and disappointment.

God may give us just what John 16:24 says He will give. Joy. Joy that we might be complete . . . whatever our circumstances.[2]

Can you say that same thing? Does your prayer life include desiring God's will no matter how difficult that may be? This is the truth about God's answers: What may seem difficult produces joy when we accept His will for us. When we turn away from His answer, what seems easy for the moment turns into more difficulties. And the greatest reward for saying yes to God's answers to our prayers is that He builds our inner self with His source of healing and strength, just as He did for Joni.

Developing a Prayer Life

Some simple steps can help you develop a lifestyle of prayer. I encourage you to keep a prayer list on which you record the date, prayer request, the date the request was answered, and your praises and thanksgiving to God. Keep your list with your devotional material, so you will use it every day.

Your list will perform three functions for you:

First, it will remind you of requests, praises, and thanks that you need to offer to God.

Second, it will help you keep your praises, thanksgiving, and requests balanced so that you don't become a "gimme" Christian and neglect giving God the honor and gratitude He deserves. You can use your "date answered" column as part of your "thank You" list.

Third, recording answers to prayer will encourage you in your walk with God. How many times have you prayed for something, received an answer, but forgotten you had even asked God for it? That happens to all of us if we're not careful to acknowledge His role in our lives. Recording requests and the date answered will help you avoid this omission. And when you become discouraged because it doesn't seem as if God is answering a specific request, you can look back to see how God has worked on your behalf in the past.

How many times have you prayed for something, received an answer, but forgotten you had even asked God for it?

Your prayer list will also help you to pray specifically. By His example and teaching, Jesus encourages us to present God with specific requests—those that have to do with our needs, our relationships, or anything that concerns us. If we do not ask for specific things, how can we expect God to answer specifically?

God delights in listening to us express our desires to Him. Prayers do not have to be long, nor does a person need to be superspiritual to talk to God. He just wants us to pour our hearts out to Him so that He can heal, soothe, and deal with our inner needs. Never be afraid to bring your deepest desires to Him because He always handles them with utmost care. You may want to use a journal to write out prayers that express your desires to God.

Find your own special times and places to pray. It is not necessary to be in any particular position to pray. I find some of my greatest times of communication with the Lord are when I'm working with my hands and my mind is free to concentrate on talking to Christ. God wants to be a part of the pattern of your life!

But do allot time first thing in the morning to talk to God and read your Bible. That will help you begin your day in the right attitude and in the power of the Spirit.

For this reason Bill and I established the habit of praying together before getting out of bed in the morning. This practice was invaluable to us in keeping our communication open with God and with each other. You can't pray with someone if there is conflict between you. Therefore, we talked out our differences and made sure we heard each other. We went to bed in love and awakened the same way the next morning.

The Butterfly Pin

I could tell you about awesome answers to prayer that I have seen God accomplish in the ministry, my life, and the lives of others. I'm sure you have received some miraculous answers also. Let me tell you one of the most unusual, intimate prayers I quickly tossed up to God. The request wasn't about an earth-shattering problem, but the answer did help me to trust God for little things as well as big ones.

One afternoon as I was dressing for a speaking engagement, I put on a new dress and realized that it needed a piece of jewelry to complement it. While searching through my jewelry box, I came across a silver butterfly pin. Because my dress was black, trimmed in gold, I thought, *A gold butterfly pin would be perfect.*

A butterfly is one of my favorite symbols because it highlights the transformation of an ugly caterpillar into a gorgeous creature that has gained access to the sky. To me, that is a reminder of my new life in Christ. Jesus has changed me from my old sinful state into an eternal creation. Since I make it a habit to pray about everything, I said, "Lord, help me find a gold butterfly to go with the dress." But I had to settle for putting on a colorful scarf.

Later that evening after I had spoken, a friend approached me with an emerald-green box. "Vonette," she said, "my husband and I bought something for you."

When I opened the box, I saw the most exquisite piece of jewelry resting on velvet. It was a gold, jeweled butterfly! The intimacy and love shown in God's answer to my prayer touched me to the depth of my soul. No one knew I had asked God for a gold butterfly! And I had asked only for a gold butterfly, but this one had little rubies, sapphires, emeralds, and even two little diamonds, all individually set. From that pin I learned a great spiritual lesson: If God is interested enough to provide a butterfly pin, He is more eager to give us our large requests, especially our concerns about the spiritual needs of others.

Ephesians 3:20 says, "Now glory be to God! By his mighty

power at work within us, he is able to accomplish infinitely more than we would ever dare to ask or hope." Verse 21 gives us the ultimate purpose for His rich gifts: "May he be given glory in the church and in Christ Jesus forever and ever through endless ages. Amen." Our answers to prayer glorify God and Jesus Christ to others!

I tell you the butterfly story, not to encourage you to ask for wealth or fame or material possessions, but to show how precious God considers each prayer we send to Him. And He answers each request individually.

In fact, I have learned to pray about everything! When unexpected guests come and I don't know what to serve, I pray, "Lord, show me what to do!" Or when I'm baking and I'm out of an ingredient, I'll ask God to show me what to substitute. One day I was preparing for an evangelistic dinner party when I ran out of sauce that needed to marinate overnight. I prayed, "God, give me a creative mind!"

Instead of the original fresh tomato base for the dish, I duplicated the taste with canned goods and spices I had in my pantry, and the dish worked just as well. This may seem like a small thing to ask God about, but remember that to our mighty God even our greatest problem is a "small" thing. And He longs to hear from us about everything!

The Battle Is the Lord's

I must warn you that developing a consistent, faith-based prayer life is a constant battle. Though we must be prepared for spiritual conflict, we must also remember that our battle is the Lord's. Read this warning from God to an Old Testament king who faced an overwhelming enemy: "Listen, King Jehoshaphat! Listen, all you people of Judah and Jerusalem! This is what the Lord says: Do not be afraid! Don't be discouraged by this mighty army, for the battle is not yours, but God's" (2 Chronicles 20:15).

Why is this life sometimes so difficult and challenging to live? The greatest reason for the difficulties we face each day is just a lack of understanding about who God is. Yes, we make choices that can create problems, and these are of our own doing, but when we surrender our lives to Him, He can control our response to the consequences.

Remember, you received Christ Jesus as Lord by faith. That is how you must pray—by faith. Don't fight the spiritual battle alone. Count on God. Step over the threshold and experience real, true joy!

FOURTEEN

Ultimate Caregiving

$\mathcal{H}$ave you noticed that what the world thinks about servant-hood is a far cry from what the Bible teaches?

At times the world tries to implement the Bible's wisdom on serving others, but it fails miserably. Here is a good example: We call people who work for the federal government "public servants." Yet if you have had to deal with many of these "servants," you soon realize that they don't consider it an honor to serve the public. When you call about a matter, you often will talk to someone who is impatient with you or who gives you the runaround.

Think of the people in our society who are heaped with honor. Most are proud celebrities who have little time for the "regular people." I think of movie and sports superstars riding around in limousines, CEOs who aim for business profits at the expense of their employees, politicians who pass laws to benefit themselves even when it hurts the country as a whole.

Of course, I have known many public servants, sports figures, business executives, and politicians who were godly and self-lessly served others. But they are the exceptions in our society.

In God's kingdom serving others is the way to achieve honor. I can relate to the way the disciples stumbled over this simple truth. They were wondering who was going to be the greatest in heaven. As you can imagine, their motives for asking this question were not pure! Jesus called over a small child and explained that the greatest in the kingdom were those who became like little children in humility and service to God.

Not long after this lesson, mothers and fathers brought their children to Jesus so He could bless them. After the object lesson the disciples had just heard, you'd think they would have been overjoyed to see the ones Jesus considered great. Instead, the disciples rebuked those who had brought the children to Jesus, trying to send them away.

Jesus was irritated by the disciples' action. He said, "Let the children come to me. Don't stop them! For the Kingdom of God belongs to such as these" (Mark 10:14).

Later, a rich man came up to Jesus and wanted to know how he could have eternal life. Jesus told him to give away his wealth and follow Him. The man went away, not willing to change his heart.

The disciples were astounded. They were sure that the rich were on the inside track to heaven. But Jesus said the opposite. He gave this momentous teaching: "Many who seem to be important now will be the least important then, and those who are considered least here will be the greatest then" (Matthew 19:30).

In God's eyes those who serve others are greater than those who serve themselves. Jesus provided the perfect model: He served us by living on earth and dying for our sins. He tells us, "For even I, the Son of Man, came here not to be served but to serve others, and to give my life as a ransom for many" (Matthew 20:28). With Jesus as our example, how can we do less?

Role Reversal

God's plan for serving was turned upside down even before the world was created. The problem began in Satan's heart. He had been created with honor and beauty, yet that wasn't good enough for him. He decided that he could be better than his own Creator. So rather than serving God, he rebelled against Him and started a chain reaction that has led to sin and death (Isaiah 14:12-15). God created Satan to worship and serve Him, but instead Satan served himself.

Since the days of the Garden of Eden, Satan has been tempting men and women to serve themselves rather than God. We can see this same role reversal at work first in Adam and Eve. Rather than obeying God, they sinned by helping themselves to the forbidden fruit. They put their desires ahead of their obligation to serve God. As a result, they reaped pain and death and expulsion from their beautiful garden. They missed out on the glorious communion they once had with their Creator and the joy of serving Him.

That same attitude has infected humankind since. It's called our sin nature. It encourages us to put ourselves first and God and others second. The role of being a servant just doesn't come naturally to us.

But when Christ came to live within us at our spiritual birth, He gave us a new nature so that servanthood became our inner desire. This role is what the Holy Spirit wants to develop in us.

In contrast to Satan's sin is God's own example of submission. Although the three persons of the Trinity are equal in every way, Jesus submitted Himself to the Father in all things. In the garden of Gethsemane, when He was preparing for the agony of the cross, He said, "Father, if you are willing, please take this cup of suffering away from me. Yet I want your will, not mine" (Luke 22:42).

In the same way, the Holy Spirit has come into the world not to do His own will but to do the Father's will—to glorify the Son (John 16:13-14). Do you see the pattern? Serving and submissiveness are in the heart of God. That is the spirit that He desires to build into our lives. As we serve Him, we will want to serve others, thereby imitating the life of Christ.

Serving Others

In earlier chapters we discussed serving God by surrendering all that we are to Him and to His will. This leads us to serving others because that is God's will for us.

The more I rely upon the enabling power of the Holy Spirit, the more He gives me the ability to be used by God in the lives of others.

Within a glass case in a palace in Genoa, Italy, lies the violin of the great violinist Paganini. It was given to the city to be kept as a treasure, with the instruction that it was never to be played upon again. This instrument, so highly prized that it is kept under guard, at one time uplifted the souls of thousands with its matchless music as it yielded itself to the master's touch. But now, not only is its life of usefulness at an end, it soon may become a heap of dust. Because of the character of the wood, with the lack of human touch, the violin has become the victim of tiny insects that are rapidly causing its decay. What was created to produce lovely music is wasting away.

As we yield our lives to our Master, God uses us as His instruments to demonstrate His power. God has given His children a free will to obey or disobey His commands. The apostle Paul pleads, "For you have been called to live in freedom—not freedom to satisfy your sinful nature, but freedom to serve one another in love" (Galatians 5:13). This, then, is the mark of love—that we are serving God and others.

Sometimes, however, we feel inadequate to serve others. What do we say when a friend's husband dies suddenly in an accident? How can we help that child whose heart is broken by her parents' divorce? What can we do for our pastor when he is under a tremendous load of responsibility?

When God tells us in Romans 6:13 to submit our bodies to Him as instruments of righteousness, He is saying, "Present yourselves to Me. Make yourselves available. I want to work through you." It's when we feel the most inadequate that we most rely on God. As we do, He gives us the wisdom and strength to serve. We may not have the right words to say or do the best actions, but the Holy Spirit will use us to shine His love and comfort into hurting hearts.

You may tend to be overwhelmed by what you need to accomplish or be haunted by a past failure, but I encourage you to draw from that Source offered by your Creator. Allow the Holy Spirit to bring to your mind some ideas of ways you can help a neighbor or friend. You will be surprised by how much you can accomplish when you allow God to work through you.

I am aware that many women discount my advice by saying, "Well, I'm not married to Bill Bright. I could never do these things." Every woman is a unique creation, and God has a plan tailored just for you. He brings specific people into your sphere of influence. You have an imprint on your life that equips you to serve God in just the way He desires. My goal in writing this book is to help you understand the importance of serving others through a life filled by the Holy Spirit.

We have complete assurance from the Bible that God made each of us for His glory and purpose, just as He made Jeremiah the prophet the way he was for His special purpose: "I knew you before I formed you in your mother's womb. Before you were born I set you apart and appointed you as my spokesman to the world" (Jeremiah 1:5).

My goal in writing this book is to help you understand the importance of serving others through a life filled by the Holy Spirit.

Through our service to others, God wants us to influence our world for Him. But when we look at our circumstances and the society in which we live, we may feel overwhelmed and consider our influence insignificant.

Many of the prophets of the Old Testament and disciples in the New Testament felt much the same way. When God had called Moses to lead the people out of Egypt and into the Promised Land, Moses argued, "Oh, Lord, I'm just not a good speaker. I never have been, and I'm not now, even after you have spoken to me. I'm clumsy with words" (Exodus 4:10). In Exodus 4:14 we are told that God was displeased with Moses' response.

God is also displeased with our excuses. When God gives us an idea for a task or the guidelines to perform it, we may be tempted to say, "I don't have the ability" or "Someone else is much more capable."

It was obvious from the men God chose to do His work that He did not need their abilities. When God calls us to a task and we make ourselves available to Him, it is His responsibility to give us the ability to handle the circumstances, to provide the finances, to do whatever is necessary to accomplish the task. Serving is our spiritual occupation, and we need to be as committed to that as we are to any secular activity we undertake.

Admittedly, serving can sometimes be difficult and without rewards. Whenever you live with someone, tensions can arise. I have described how much Henrietta Mears meant to me and how much I admired her. But at times I just didn't have a submissive spirit. I remember one occasion while we lived in the Bel Air house when guests arrived unexpectedly in the midst of an already overcrowded schedule. Often, after seating guests, Miss Mears would find me wherever I was working and ask, "Honey, would you mind serving a little pot of tea to the committee meeting?"

Sometimes I happily replied, "I'd love to," but in my heart I was muttering, *Why doesn't she get her own cup of tea?* At that moment, I was letting a wrong attitude dampen my joy, and if I let my mind stew, I could even put a damper on my close relationship with Henrietta. As I turned my feelings over to God, I found that my response was a genuine "I would be happy to"—even if I was inconvenienced. I was available to be used by God.

Through many circumstances like this one, over the years, I learned to accept interruptions and previously irritating situations as God's way of showing me the flaws in my servant attitude. Little by little I began to experience the reality of the Christ-controlled life as I continued to walk in His Spirit.

Let me caution those of you who tend to be weak in setting boundaries. Being Christ's servant to others doesn't mean letting people take undue advantage of you over and over. That is not in their best interest or yours. If you feel that someone may be asking more of you than is healthy, ask God to show you how to serve that person without harming your own well-being or hers. Remember that Jesus occasionally sent the crowds away so that He could be alone. His life was one of godliness and balance.

Serving Your Husband

There is a popular, romantic idea that God made one man and one woman just for each other. I choose to believe that. I'm sure that Bill Bright was made for me and that I was made for him. At the same time I quickly learned that the art of being happily married consists of more than finding the right person. If we want to have a happy home, we must each be the person God intends us to be.

Of course, in any home, the first priority must be to love and serve our Lord and to walk in the Spirit daily. Without putting God first, we cannot establish a righteous home.

As wives, our second priority is to our husbands (Ephesians 5:22-24). Because of the intimate and exclusive nature of the marriage relationship, God gives us important commands to help ensure a fulfilling relationship. As long as both partners put God first, their union will flourish. As wives, when we obey God's Word, our influence in our husbands' lives will help them realize greater fulfillment.

God tells husbands and wives to serve each other (Ephesians 5:21), and in the next verse, wives are told specifically to submit to their husbands. Implied is the word *voluntarily*, which means not with resignation, resentment, or gritted teeth but willingly from the heart. Just as with our obedience to Jesus Christ, we are to have the right heart attitude—not just outward obedience but true inward submission.

There is also a special instruction given to husbands about loving their wives (Ephesians 5:25-33). The word implied here is *sacrificially*, just as Christ loved the church.

If only husbands and wives could understand this concept before marriage and immediately begin to apply it to their commitment to each other, marriages could be strengthened. It is easy for a husband to love his wife "sacrificially" when the wife submits to her husband "voluntarily."

However, if our husband doesn't love us this way, it does not relieve us of our responsibility. We must willingly submit to our husband as to the Lord.

The world recoils at this scriptural principle. But as we have seen, submitting and serving each other is an honored role in God's kingdom. It is a measure of our greatness.

God has a practical reason for creating this order in the

family. No organization functions well without someone to act as the final authority. Let's look at how this principle works in business. Each company must have a president or CEO, someone who is responsible for final decisions. The organization would break down if workers could supersede the decisions of the CEO. On the other hand, any CEO who abuses his position and doesn't take care of his employees isn't seeing well to his business.

Every marriage relationship requires a good bit of compromise and concession, but no matter how well a relationship progresses, couples will experience differences of opinion. When we submit to our husband's authority on ultimate decisions, we protect our family. I like the way *The Living Bible* paraphrases 1 Peter 3:1: "Wives, fit in with your husbands' plans." I am sure you can describe ways in which "fitting in" is difficult. As we choose to obey God by serving our husbands, we are available to let God work through us. Obedience to God-given authority results in special blessing.

The following example makes me chuckle. A friend, whose husband is a doctor, is a petite, feminine woman. Her husband loves to ride motorcycles because it offers him release from the pressures of his medical practice. One day he asked his wife to join him.

In obedience to Scripture, she put aside her fear and learned to ride. Soon after, they made a several-hundred-mile trip together on their motorcycles. Since then, they have taken trips to visit their children at college. She now declares that they are having the time of their lives!

Right now, you may be thinking, *Vonette, you don't know my husband! He is so difficult to serve!* Remember that Jesus served those who didn't deserve it. He even washed the feet of Judas! God tells us to love our husbands in spite of their faults and sins. God has an unending supply of love and wisdom that we can draw upon to help us in any difficult situation—even that of an unbelieving spouse.

Serving Our Children

As women we have an easier time serving our children than we do our husbands. God has provided us with nurturing instincts that help us tremendously in parenting.

Because a mother is the cohesive factor in the family, she has many responsibilities. If you are a single mother, this is even more true of your parenting role. When a mother only halfheartedly attends to the well-being of her children, she leaves them open to the corrupting influences of the world. This is especially the case during the difficult teen years. I encourage you to serve your children by being available for them, listening to their problems, and teaching them responsibility—even when you are weary.

Perhaps the biggest temptation we face as mothers is to offer our children tangible things rather than our personal attention because giving of ourselves requires special effort in a busy world. There were many times in my work in Campus Crusade when I had to reevaluate what I was doing so that I didn't neglect our sons.

In every stage of our children's development, we need to consider how we can best serve them so that they will grow physically, mentally, socially, and most important, spiritually.

Their needs will constantly change, so we will need to alter our parenting approaches accordingly. But the Bible gives us eternal principles to follow. Meditate on Proverbs 13:24; 19:18; 22:6; 23:13-14; and Ephesians 6:4 to search God's mind for your parenting.

Now that our sons are grown, I find new ways to serve them without intruding on their marriage relationships. It's a joy to see how God can use me in their lives and in the lives of their wives and children.

I encourage you to pray like this: "God, I'm available for Your use. Enable me to influence my children correctly. Help me mentor them to have Christ's servant attitude too."

Women are free to choose what they want to do, yet the woman seeking God's heart will find freedom in serving others. And do you want to know a secret? In serving, we uncover the greatest fulfillment within and become a stellar example of a woman who knows and loves Jesus. Particularly if we have chosen to be married and to have children, the responsibilities we have assumed confine us to some boundaries for a few years but offer the greatest rewards that can possibly be realized.

One area of service to others that is vital is sharing our faith. In the next chapter we will learn what God expects of us and how He will lead us to bring others into His kingdom.

In serving we uncover the greatest fulfillment within and become a stellar example of a woman who knows and loves Jesus.

FIFTEEN

A Secret to Tell

If you have grandchildren, like I do, you know the pure joy of telling people about them. There's nothing like relating a story of what my grandsons have said or what my granddaughters have accomplished! Have you ever listened to a young woman who is engaged to marry the godly man she loves? The details of how well he treats her flood her conversation. Sometimes we can be so full of joy in our relationships that we couldn't possibly keep quiet about them.

When we have a dynamic relationship with God, this same principle is at work. Our hearts will be so full of joy, love, and gratitude about what God has done for us that we can't keep the news to ourselves. We want our friends to know and experience this spiritual relationship that has transformed our life. Paul explains our response: "Everywhere we go, we tell everyone about Christ. We warn them and teach them with all the wisdom God has

There is no thrill quite as wonderful as seeing someone come to trust Christ because I have been faithful in sharing my faith!

given us, for we want to present them to God, perfect in their relationship to Christ" (Colossians 1:28). There is no thrill quite as wonderful as seeing someone come to trust Christ because I have been faithful in sharing my faith!

God's Command to Share

We share our life in Christ with others out of hearts overflowing with gratitude, but also because Jesus commanded us to do so. We won't always feel like telling others about Jesus, but we should be obedient despite our emotions.

A person's last words are usually significant. Do you recall what Jesus said just before He ascended to heaven? His words are found in Acts 1:8: "When the Holy Spirit has come upon you, you will receive power and will tell people about me everywhere—in Jerusalem, throughout Judea, in Samaria, and to the ends of the earth." This is a command for Jesus' followers—those in the first century as well as us today—to spread His message everywhere in the power of the Holy Spirit.

As a new believer I wanted to tell others about Jesus, but I was afraid that I couldn't do well because I wasn't familiar with the Bible. Then I read 1 John 1:3, "Again I say, we are telling you about what we ourselves have actually seen and heard, so that you may share the fellowship and the joys we have with the Father and with Jesus Christ his Son" (TLB). Suddenly I realized that all I had to do was share what I had seen and heard or what God had revealed to me at that point in my life. As I obeyed God, I discovered that many people were looking for answers I had found. Even though I didn't know a lot about the Bible, people were interested in what had happened to me. That was a jumping-off point to telling them about God's gift of love and forgiveness.

Today when I'm alone with a person for more than five minutes, I make it a practice to pursue a conversation about that person's spiritual interests. I try to identify with her in some way that will give us common ground on which to base our conversation.

Once we can share what God has done for us, we can use a witnessing tool to help us share our faith more effectively. One tool that I use frequently is *The Four Spiritual Laws*. Sometimes I begin by asking, "Have you seen this little booklet? The concepts in it have changed my life." After opening the conversation, I simply read through the booklet with the person. The text gives questions to ask at the appropriate places and a prayer the person can use to express her heartfelt desire to receive Christ as Savior. An adaptation of *The Four Spiritual Laws*, "Beginning Your Journey of Joy," is reprinted in the back of this book. Also, your church or other Christian organizations may offer training in how to share your faith.

In some situations I only have time to hand *The Four Spiritual Laws* booklet to someone and share that these truths have changed my life. I encourage that person to read the booklet on her own and consider its message.

Our Opportunities

As we yield ourselves to the Holy Spirit and share our faith, it's amazing to see the way God will open doors for us to present the gospel and give us the ability to identify with the person with whom we're sharing.

One of the most intriguing experiences I've had in sharing my faith was with a young woman who was en route to Omaha, Nebraska. I was flying from New Orleans to Minneapolis, and the flight had been a long one—eight hours with three stops. I had already had two seat partners and had shared my faith with both of them. They had been extremely interested, but neither had received Christ. After the second woman left the plane, I was ready to rest. But I did pray that if God wanted me to share my faith again, I was willing.

Just before the plane took off, a cute blonde girl in feminine clothes plopped into the seat next to mine. In an irritated voice she said, "Well, if this plane gets off the ground, it will be a miracle! This is the third plane I have boarded, and the other two planes had mechanical problems."

I responded, "Well, I have something for you that will show you why God has put you on this plane." I was amazed at my own words, but I handed her something called the "Van Dusen Letter" that gives a presentation of the gospel similar to *The Four Spiritual Laws.*

After reading a few sentences, she asked sharply, "Where did you get this?"

I explained that my husband had written it to a businessman to explain how a person can become a Christian.

"Why did you share this with me?"

"I asked God to send the right person to sit next to me."

As she continued reading the letter, she often paused to make comments. "This is fantastic." "I can't believe you'd give this to me." "This answers my questions." "I always wanted to know about this."

After she finished reading, she quietly said, "God did put me here beside you on this plane."

She told me that she had gone to a fashionable girls' school where her morals had plummeted. She had done almost everything. She had been engaged several times, but each relationship had been broken off. Now there was another man in her life. She said, "If this relationship doesn't work out, I'll have absolutely nothing to live for."

That day, as we talked, she prayed to ask Christ into her life!

For the next several months I received letters from her. She said that she shared the Van Dusen Letter with her boyfriend, and he had prayed to receive Christ. He then suggested that she share the letter with his mother. When she did, they found out that his mother was a Christian and had been praying for them.

In her last letter to me she said that she and her boyfriend were planning to marry and establish a godly home.

God's Responsibility in Our Witnessing

I have met many women who feel discouraged after sharing their faith with someone who didn't respond positively. Not everyone with whom I share Christ places her trust in Him. Many people are not ready to make an intelligent decision for Christ, or they are involved in a sinful lifestyle and don't want to turn their life over to Him. I have learned that whatever reasons may prevent a person from responding in faith, my responsibility is to share

Christ in the power of the Holy Spirit and leave the results to God.

Do you see the principles in this statement?

1. I make myself available to share my faith.
2. I make sure I am filled with the Holy Spirit.
3. God is responsible for the results.

In my experience on the plane, I was available to God and asked Him for the opportunity to share. I was prepared with a gospel presentation that made sharing my faith easier. When the first two women left without making a decision for Christ, I left them in God's hands. He is sovereign, and He can remind them, long after our meeting, of what they heard. God also knew their hearts.

The third opportunity became such a joy for me. God knew that this girl was ready to listen, and He worked out the circumstances so we could sit beside each other.

Perhaps you are the type of person who finds it hard to speak up about your faith. Does the thought of bringing up a spiritual topic make your knees weak? God can help you overcome your fear. As women, we can approach witnessing in a more relational manner, gently probing the spiritual well-being of another person and sensing where that person stands before the Lord. But remember this: the disciples practiced their faith "in season and out of season." They weren't afraid to proclaim the message of Jesus Christ even with the threat of their lives. Their boldness, produced by the Holy Spirit, was why the first-century church grew so rapidly even amid persecution. So many people we meet don't experience the joy we have. By relying on the Holy Spirit, we, too, must spread the joyful news at every opportunity—whether we find it easy or not!

Be Faithful

In all the years that I have been sharing my faith, not one witnessing situation has been exactly like another. That's because God sees each person as an individual with unique personality and situation. God meets each of us where we are.

Becky Tirabassi is the author of a well-received book, *Wild Things Happen When I Pray*. When Becky and her husband moved into a new neighborhood, she learned her neighbors' names right away. She wrote them in her prayer journal and prayed for each one every day. As a young woman she had committed herself to pray for one hour a day, and she still keeps this commitment. She prayed that her neighbors would learn about God's love and then trust in Jesus Christ.

But Becky wasn't putting action to her prayers. She wasn't looking for opportunities to share the gospel. In fact, she thought God would hear her prayers and then lead her neighbors to *other* Christians in their lives. And then *they'd* invite them to church and witness to *her* neighbors.

One day, after more than three years of praying for her neighbors by name, Becky was listening to Pastor Charles Stanley's radio program, *In Touch*.

One sentence in Dr. Stanley's message pierced Becky's heart. He said, "Don't pray about anything you wouldn't want God to do through you." Becky began to realize that she just might be the very one God would want to use in the lives of her neighbors.

When Becky's neighbor Barbara knocked on her door a few days later, Becky began putting action to her prayers. First, she told Barbara how she prayed for her daily. Then she invited her to church. As they became more acquainted, they talked often about church, God, and faith. Eventually, Barbara placed her faith in Christ.

I could tell you many more stories of witnessing from my life and the lives of others. God does answer our prayers and use us to lead others to faith in Christ! You have seen how God works in your life. The answers to prayer you have received, the guidance for the future, the comfort during difficult times are all tailor-made just for you. Therefore, you can be sure that God will use your availability in sharing your faith as a unique, joyful experience for both you and the person He leads you to. You may not always see immediate results, but all God wants is your obedience and faithfulness.

You may not always see immediate results, but all God wants is your obedience and faithfulness.

You can expect difficulties at times. A college football player spent the spring break week partying on a Florida beach. One day a petite female college student he had never met came up to him and shared her faith. In his partially drunken state, he made fun of her and rejected her message. She went away thinking she had made little impact on him.

But her mention of Jesus remained with the football player. In time he investigated the claims of Jesus Christ and received Him

as his Savior. How he wished then that he knew the girl's name
so he could tell her what her witness had meant to him.

I encourage you to be available to God to spread His message
of love to everyone you meet. The experiences you have will
enrich your life. Let His Spirit guide you both in learning how to
give a simple gospel presentation and in seeing opportunities to
share His love and forgiveness with those He brings your way.

Use Your Skills

Ethel Wilcox, who taught me so much about the Holy Spirit,
related a story about a major railroad accident that resulted in
serious injury to scores of passengers. The badly injured were
laid in rows along the track awaiting the arrival of doctors and
ambulances from a nearby town. A young woman, frantic at the
cries of the sufferers, walked helplessly along the line. Suddenly
she recognized her own physician standing motionless, his head
bent low. Amazed to see him standing there doing nothing, she
shook his arm and screamed at him, "Do something! Why don't
you do something?"

Lifting his head, he exclaimed, "Do something? Why don't I
do something? Young woman, I'm helpless. I can do nothing.
I have no instruments!"

We need never be like this doctor, our hands empty of instruments. God is willing to build the skills into our lives that will be
like instruments, enabling us to heal the spiritually sick in this
world as we depend on His Spirit's power. God freely gives the
skills as we ask and apply them to our lives.

The life of a Christian woman is a full and joyful adventure. God will be faithful to build into your life all the spiritual skills you need to enable you to live to the max. He will guide you into His will and help you bear spiritual fruit. His Spirit will show you truths from God's Word and will deepen your communion with Him through prayer. The Spirit will equip you to serve others in your home, neighborhood, and workplace, and in the ministry that God lays on your heart. And as you walk daily in His Spirit, God will open many avenues for you to share your faith.

Knowing that God will help you acquire all these skills, doesn't it give you a feeling of confidence and purpose? Those who don't allow God to direct every part of their lives just can't imagine what they are missing! The pathway of obedience can sometimes be difficult, but it always leads to a strengthening of our inner woman.

With these godly skills in mind, we can go on to complete the work that God intends for our lives. We will uncover the truths in God's Word about achieving our spiritual purpose in life.

PART 4

ACHIEVING HIS PURPOSE

---

*I have fought a good fight, I have finished the race, and
I have remained faithful. And now the prize awaits me—
the crown of righteousness that the Lord, the righteous
Judge, will give me on that great day of his return. And
the prize is not just for me but for all who eagerly
look forward to his glorious return.*

2 TIMOTHY 4:7-8

Let me share in Thy works not asking

that I must see the results in my day,

but laboring in this confidence because

it was done in Thee it will someday

come to fulfillment and I will not have

lived worthlessly, selfishly, needlessly.

BOB BENSON,
LAUGHTER IN THE WALLS

SIXTEEN
Growing Up Gracefully

One of the most memorable events of the 1984 Olympic Games in Los Angeles was the 20K walk. The race included several laps in the coliseum, then a distance around the city streets, and finally a lap in the coliseum.

Soon after the start of the race, a competitor from Costa Rica, Herman Carazo, fell significantly behind. Nonetheless, he kept walking as fast as he could. The others, on their subsequent laps, caught up to him and passed him as he walked his first laps in the coliseum.

When all the other walkers had completed their coliseum laps, they headed out to the city streets to complete that portion of the race. When everyone else had gone, Carazo still had two laps to go inside the coliseum. As this lone walker circled the track two more times, 100,000 pairs of eyes watched him.

He kept on walking. The crowd began to cheer. There was a shared sense of joy—pride even—that this one person, in the midst of a massive crowd, would stay in the race.

At first, the spectators had cheered for their own countrymen. Now they were united for this lone walker. They cheered, clapped, waved flags, and even chanted, "Costa Rica! Costa Rica!"

The cheering faded as he disappeared from the coliseum into the city streets to try to catch up with his competition.

Later the walkers returned for their final lap in the coliseum. All the other racers completed their laps, and the medals were awarded.

Then, much later, a figure appeared in the coliseum tunnel. It was the Costa Rican walker. Almost two and a half hours after the race had begun, Carazo finished his final lap.

The entire crowd stood to their feet and cheered. He crossed the finish line! Then he collapsed. An ambulance arrived and picked him up. Instead of discretely slipping out of the coliseum, the ambulance circled in a victory lap. In unison, the crowd cheered again.

What this walker had achieved was not the fastest race, but a race of endurance. Even when he knew that he would be last, he persevered. His satisfaction came from the fact that he had finished the race he had set out to walk.

We are also in a race—a spiritual one. Paul describes our effort in this way:

As a result, I can really know Christ and experience the mighty power that raised him from the dead. I can learn what it means to suffer with him, sharing in his death, so that, somehow, I can experience the resurrection from the dead! I don't mean to say that I have already achieved these things or that I have already reached perfection! But I keep working toward that day when I will finally be all that Christ Jesus saved me for and wants me to be. No, dear brothers and sisters, I am still not all I should be, but I am focusing all my energies on this one thing: Forgetting the past and looking forward to what lies ahead, I strain to reach the end of the race and receive the prize for which God, through Christ Jesus, is calling us up to heaven. (Philippians 3:10-14)

In the beginning we admitted our need to God and became a member of His family. Then we learned how to accept His grace so that we could live fulfilled lives within the parameters of His standards and will for us. Then we discovered how to acquire skills that will enable us to be fruitful in God's kingdom. Now we turn our attention to achieving His purpose for our lives. Whatever that purpose is, we strain to reach it with the faithfulness and endurance of that Costa Rican runner.

Ralph W. Sockman writes, "The true believer in the Holy Spirit is one who knows how to hoist the sail of his own spirit to catch the winds of God."[1] Friend, we cannot look at the failures we have experienced or the sin to which we succumbed. Instead, we set our eyes on the finish line, forgetting the past, and straining toward the mark of spiritual maturity and fruitfulness.

We set our eyes on the finish line, forgetting the past, and straining toward the mark of spiritual maturity and fruitfulness.

What is our goal, the one thing we are to focus all our energies on? Paul writes, "I once thought all these things were so very important, but now I consider them worthless because of what Christ has done. Yes, everything else is

worthless when compared with the priceless gain of knowing
Christ Jesus my Lord. I have discarded everything else, counting
it all as garbage, so that I may have Christ and become one with
him. I no longer count on my own goodness or my ability to obey
God's law, but I trust Christ to save me. For God's way of making
us right with himself depends on faith" (Philippians 3:7-9).

Spiritual Maturity

One of the marks of spiritual maturity is a consistent,
Spirit-controlled life. I have met so many women who have let
the fortunes of life control them. Sometimes it can be extremely
difficult to hold fast to God's standards and will for our lives.

I think of one woman whose husband had left her for another
woman. They had been married for more than twenty years, and
his rejection left her devastated. She found that God was close to
her during this emotional crisis, but a few years after her divorce,
she still felt a hunger for a relationship with a man. Instead of
turning this need over to God for His comfort and wisdom, she
began dating a man who was not living close to God. In fact, even
though he professed to be a Christian, she wasn't sure because
she didn't see any spiritual fruit in his life.

This relationship caused her all kinds of harm. She began to
miss church services, and her devotional life suffered. She no
longer saw her Christian friends much because she was afraid of
what they would say about her involvement with this man. And
she has been a poor example for her teenage children.

We can get off track with God during both good and bad

circumstances. We can all fall into the temptation of trying to live from one high experience to another. There is nothing wrong with rejoicing when we get a pay raise or celebrating when our son or daughter graduates from high school. But these experiences shouldn't shape our walk with God. They should be times of thanking Him for the good things He has provided and a way to focus even more closely on His love for us.

In the same way, our low points shouldn't affect how we handle life. What do you do when a friend betrays you? Perhaps even your husband? Of course, God expects us to cry and feel sorrow about events that pierce our hearts. Jesus wept at the tomb of Lazarus and cried out to His Father in the garden of Gethsemane. But difficult times shouldn't change our desire to be near to God and to walk with Him. In fact, both good times and bad should show us how much we need to rely on Him in every circumstance.

God expects a spiritually mature person to exhibit certain characteristics:

- *Behave like a spiritual grownup.* "It's like this: When I was a child, I spoke and thought and reasoned as a child does. But when I grew up, I put away childish things" (1 Corinthians 13:11).
- *Think like a spiritual grownup.* "Dear brothers and sisters, don't be childish in your understanding of these things. Be innocent as babies when it comes to evil, but be mature and wise in understanding matters of this kind" (1 Corinthians 14:20).
- *Minister and relate to other believers like a spiritual grownup.* "Their responsibility is to equip God's people to do his

work and build up the church, the body of Christ, until we come to such unity in our faith and knowledge of God's Son that we will be mature and full grown in the Lord, measuring up to the full stature of Christ" (Ephesians 4:12-13).

- *Study the Bible like a spiritual grownup.* "You have been Christians a long time now, and you ought to be teaching others. Instead, you need someone to teach you again the basic things a beginner must learn about the Scriptures. You are like babies who drink only milk and cannot eat solid food. And a person who is living on milk isn't very far along in the Christian life and doesn't know much about doing what is right. Solid food is for those who are mature, who have trained themselves to recognize the difference between right and wrong and then do what is right" (Hebrews 5:12-14).

- *Overcome temptation like a spiritual grownup.* "I have written to you who are young because you are strong with God's word living in your hearts, and you have won your battle with Satan" (1 John 2:14).

- *Love consistently like a spiritual grownup.* "Then we will no longer be like children, forever changing our minds about what we believe because someone has told us something different or because someone has cleverly lied to us and made the lie sound like the truth" (Ephesians 4:14).

- *Express contentment like a spiritual grownup.* "Stay away from the love of money; be satisfied with what you have. For God has said, 'I will never fail you. I will never forsake you'" (Hebrews 13:5).

Contentment

I find contentment is hard for me to achieve. I have a streak of perfectionism in my character, and it battles against contentment. In fact, straining toward the goal and being content seem like opposite concepts. How can we strain to reach the end of the race if we are content to be where we are?

This really is no mystery if we understand two concepts about straining toward the goal of godliness. One is that we must not desire a different goal than the one God has put before us. This is what God is telling us in Hebrews 13:5. We can easily supplant our God-given goal with a race to hoard material possessions or wealth. Then we are running a race that is not pleasing to God.

God has created humankind with an innate desire to achieve something in life. If you are not pursuing godliness, you will be running toward something else. You can see this so clearly in the lives of non-Christians. For example, think of a family who lives for recreation. They work all week just to get away on the week-end; then they go back to work on Monday thinking about the next weekend. Even if they don't acknowledge it, camping or some sport activity has become their goal. Compare this with the Christian family who camps to enjoy God's beauty and to build unity in the family. Their camping serves a bigger goal—to get to know God. And they don't let their recreation interfere with their enjoyment of work or the ministry God has given them in their church.

Bill and I also met many Christian businessmen and women who use their gift for making money in the service of the Lord. I'm sure you've met many people whose main goal in life is to retire with a huge bank account. They direct their lives around their pursuit of money. But Christian stewards have a different focus. Rather than setting a bigger bank account as their goal, they see the increase in their resources as a way to build God's kingdom. And you can see the spiritual fruit of contentment in their lives. They are first committed to God's kingdom and use their resources and time accordingly.

The second concept about straining toward the goal is that we leave our talents, abilities, and successes in God's hands. When we take upon ourselves the responsibility for gaining the prize, we lose. We can never in our human strength become or accomplish what God wants for us. But when we walk in the Spirit, allowing God to set the pace and the goal, we rest in His ability and His wisdom. That doesn't mean that we don't work hard but that we are content to let God run the show.

That Costa Rican man did not have the athletic ability to finish in the top three in his race and win a medal. He knew that when he began. But he did reach his goal—to finish the race with the best time he could make. In doing so, he brought glory to his country. Probably no one in the stands will remember his name, but they will remember that the walker from Costa Rica gave the best effort.

Our purpose is to bring glory to God, not to ourselves. So it matters not only that we finish the race but also how we run.

If we do the same for God, we have been successful. Our purpose is to bring glory to God, not to ourselves. So it matters not only that we finish the race but also how we run.

A Life of Influence

Right now I want you to list all the people in your life who are influenced by what you do. Include people such as your family, your neighbors (whether you know them or not), coworkers, your dentist and doctors, the clerks at the store where you shop, your hairdresser, the gas station attendant. How many did you name?

In one way or another, you are an influence on these people. If you snap at the supermarket cashier or the bank teller for a mistake she made, or you ignore your new neighbors and do not introduce yourself to them, you are showing them a side of you. On the other hand, if you respond lovingly when others are short with you, you show them another side. (Interesting how this corresponds to the old nature/new nature battle within us!)

One woman wanted to teach her children the importance of treating people with respect even during the stresses of Christmas shopping. She had found that many salesclerks were short-tempered during the holiday season, so she and her children made inexpensive gifts that they brought with them shopping. After they paid for their purchases, they handed the clerk a small gift and said, "Merry Christmas." It was unbelievable how that small kindness brought smiles to the faces of the harried workers!

Of course, living life with a consistent spiritual walk deeply influences those we love most. Can you imagine what would happen if you stopped yelling at the kids when your household is in chaos and took a moment to pray instead? Only God can build those kinds of responses in our lives, but that's exactly what He wants to do! You have His Spirit living in you, waiting for you to give Him permission to change the area of your life that is out of control.

One other area of your life also creates an incredible amount of influence—your ministry. Paul writes to Archippus, a member of the Colossian church, "Be sure to carry out the work the Lord gave you" (Colossians 4:17). Each of us has a role to perform in the ministry of the kingdom. That includes relaying your faith to your family, sharing your faith with others, working in your church, giving of your financial resources as God has blessed you, helping the poor and needy, building up other believers in the Word.

I am only one person, but as I have determined to apply scriptural principles to my life and have shared my knowledge with others, my life has influenced many. I have learned that it doesn't matter where I am, God will use me.

In the 1990s the leadership of Campus Crusade for Christ felt for many reasons that God was leading us to move the headquarters from Arrowhead Springs to Lake Hart in Orlando, Florida. That was a hard transition for me. Arrowhead Springs was where our sons grew up, where I had so many wonderful memories, and where Bill and I had made our home for almost thirty years.

But I knew that it isn't where God plants us that is important. To paraphrase an old adage, what's important is that you "bloom where you're planted." I have seen so many miracles and ministry opportunities happen in Orlando, and I rejoice in God's purpose for my life both in California and in Florida.

You are only one person, but as you make the same decision to achieve God's purpose where He plants you, it is possible for you to make an impact upon our world. You are essential to God's kingdom. You can achieve His purpose in your life!

SEVENTEEN

A Life That Matters

$\mathcal{I}$t was a beautiful spring day in Charlotte, North Carolina, and the warm greeting I received at the airport was just the beginning of a memorable weekend. I had been asked to speak at a graduation for a Christian high school. Of course, I was overjoyed with the invitation. Sometimes when invitations to speak come to my desk, the enemy of my soul tries to make me believe that the committee members really wanted Bill, but since he wasn't available they invited me. This was not the case this time. They really did want me to be the speaker.

My yellow linen dress was pressed and ready, and my notes were tucked in my Bible. The only glitch in the preparations came when the microphone needed to be placed inside my dress. This required a trip to the ladies room, and with the help of the pastor's wife and my associate, we maneuvered the cord up from the hem and out through the neck of my once neatly pressed dress.

As I took my place on the platform, I realized I was sitting with the faculty, the people who had invested their lives in teaching and training these young people, offering them life skills that were provided by the Holy Spirit. What a treat to be in their presence!

The faces of the family and friends radiated with the love of Christ, and the young people were like cannons with fuses lit and ready to explode into the world.

Then it was time for the official graduation speech from the valedictorian. The young woman stepped up onto the platform wearing high-heeled shoes that would make an orthopedic doctor gasp. Her long, brown hair flowed gracefully beneath her mortarboard. She confidently approached the podium, and with great poise launched into an animated greeting. You would have thought this event had been planned just for her.

Then she unexpectedly turned around, looked me in the eyes, and thanked me for coming to her graduation. "I want you to know the timeliness of your presence at my gradua-tion," she said. "My mother and father both received Christ while on college campuses through the ministry of Campus Crusade. They met at a student conference at Arrowhead Springs. Now here I am, the next generation, living out the legacy of faith."

You can't imagine how her statements made me feel. So many times we don't see the fruits of our labor, but they are there, sprout-ing and growing. Some we will never know about until we reach heaven and God shows us what He has harvested by our availabil-ity. But occasionally we get to participate in the joy of seeing some-one else's life changed because of our faithfulness to God's call. This young woman was a second generation Christian because of the vision God had given Bill and the work He had done through Bill and me and all of the staff over these many years.

The young woman's graduation address was no less exuberant as she exhorted the students of the Christian high school to never forget the blessings of the quality education they had received and to treasure the relationships made and remember the values taught. Her face glowed with enthusiasm.

Intrigued by her confident manner, my mind replayed my own high school graduation. How different the cultural climate was in my teen years! At that time I didn't even know the power of God in my life and could never have imagined what God was going to do with the girl from the little town of Coweta.

Gratitude for the many years of serving the Lord beside Bill filled my heart with confidence for the future. I could not help being thrilled, knowing that the heart of that beautiful young woman shared a similar passion with mine.

At the same time, a sad fact crossed my mind: The energy and zeal of youth is too often traded for complacency and cynicism. What happens as we mature? Why do we allow our excitement for life to become overshadowed with routine?

I would soon be addressing these bright young minds, so I prayed a silent prayer that something I would say could be used by the Holy Spirit to infuse lasting joy and excitement into their hearts to help prepare them for the future.

That's also my desire for you, my reader. I have shared some of my thoughts and experiences with you to show you how wonderful a life lived step-by-step in the power of the Holy Spirit can be. I couldn't imagine doing anything less than giving God all that I am and will be with each new day that I am privileged to experience—no matter what happens.

Our Glorious Future

I want to challenge you with the truth that God will make a miracle of your life as you allow Him to conform the woman within you to IIis Son's image. I encourage you to let God use you to glorify Him through your circumstances rather than letting your circumstances dictate what you will do. He will continue to surprise you with all that He will do in you and through you. Even after fifty years of ministry, I never know what God is going to do around the next bend in my life. We cannot predict how God will use us. This fact was reinforced recently.

God will make a miracle of your life as you allow Him to conform the woman within you to His Son's image.

One day my husband announced, "Vonette, you ought to write a novel." My husband lived his life in such total surrender to Christ that when he got a creative thought, I had no doubt about the source, so I listened carefully. But at that moment I had no idea how far the concept would take me.

We began to pursue the fiction idea, and since Bill had teamed with Ted Dekker to coauthor a novel, we knew it could be done. Through a series of discussions, the name Nancy Moser became familiar, and after I met with her, we decided our hearts and passions could blend. The writing began, and my relationship with Nancy became one of true sisters.

The first novel we wrote, *The Sister Circle*, centers around a boardinghouse and the seven women who eventually form a deep bond that cannot be broken, despite their vast differences in age, background, approaches to life, and values. *The Sister Circle* is the first in what will be a four-book series, each exploring a particular theme on love.

What was truly amazing about the book was that the main character, Evelyn, experienced just what I am experiencing as I develop these products at my mature stage in life. Evelyn was a new widow, unsure of what she should do, when God led her into a ministry to the women who moved into her boarding-house. She never dreamed how effective she could be in the kingdom at this point in her life.

That's what has happened to me. Becoming a novelist has been an unexpected joy. It has been a mind-stretching experience for me to write a nonfiction book to help you discover the real woman within while at the same time working on a fiction book exhibiting characters with vulnerabilities, strengths, and weaknesses not uncommon to most of us. But I found God to be faithful at putting all the pieces together.

I have always known that women have a delightful ability to fantasize, and as exhilarating as it may be, the rising popularity of secular romance novels and soap operas does concern me. The only conclusion I can draw is that many women are not content with life as it is, so they opt out to create in their minds a world that exists only on the pages of a book or a TV screen.

Unrealistic expectations create a perfect backdrop for disappointment and discouragement. Many women live in a state of mere existence rather than a life of joy and contentment. The problem is not in the people and events around them but rather in the hearts and souls of women who have settled for less than God's best.

The Sister Circle products, which include fiction books, nonfiction books, and Discovery Diaries, are meant to engage you in a fiction world that will give you spiritual insights and introduce you to nonfiction books that can teach you concepts of how to live abundantly.

I wish I could step into your world and sit with you, face-to-face, heart-to-heart, and share in a time of prayer. But do you realize that through the Holy Spirit we can pray together? I am writing a prayer and offering it to God as a token of my commitment to the women who read this book. Please pray it with me. Perhaps you will pray it again and again.

> *Dear loving, heavenly Father,*
>
> *Thank You for allowing me to be Your child. I feel so treasured. Please help me to accept the words of this book as a reminder of Your great and awesome love for me. I am worthy of Your love because You said I am. Remind me to honor this vessel You have created. I want to continue on with my journey of faith for the rest of my life in a way that others will recognize Your image reflected in my life. Thank You! Thank You!*
>
> *In the precious name of Jesus,*
> *Amen.*

You have a glorious future in Christ! Live every moment of it in His power and love!

Beginning Your
Journey of Joy

*T*hese four principles are essential in beginning a journey of joy.

1 — God Loves You and Created You to Know Him Personally

GOD'S LOVE "God so loved the world that He gave His one and only Son, that whoever believes in Him shall not perish but have eternal life" (John 3:16, NIV).

GOD'S PLAN "Now this is eternal life: that they may know You, the only true God, and Jesus Christ, whom You have sent" (John 17:3, NIV).

What prevents us from knowing God personally?

2 — People Are Sinful and Separated from God, So We Cannot Know Him Personally or Experience His Love

PEOPLE ARE SINFUL "All have sinned and fall short of the glory of God" (Romans 3:23, NIV).

People were created to have fellowship with God; but because of our own stubborn self-will, we chose to go our own independent way and fellowship with God was broken. This self-will, characterized by an attitude of active rebellion or passive indifference, is an evidence of what the Bible calls sin.

PEOPLE ARE SEPARATED "The wages of sin is death" [spiritual separation from God] (Romans 6:23, NIV).

This diagram illustrates that God is holy and people are sinful. A great gulf separates the two. The arrows illustrate that people are continually trying to reach God and establish a personal relationship with Him through our own efforts, such as a good life, philosophy, or religion—but we inevitably fail.

The third principle explains the only way to bridge this gulf. . . .

3 — Jesus Christ Is God's Only Provision for Our Sin. Through Him Alone We Can Know God Personally and Experience His Love

HE DIED IN OUR PLACE "God demonstrates His own love toward us, in that while we were yet sinners, Christ died for us" (Romans 5:8, NASB).

HE ROSE FROM THE DEAD "Christ died for our sins. . . . He was buried. . . . He was raised on the third day according to the Scriptures. . . . He appeared to Peter, and then to the Twelve. After that, He appeared to more than five hundred" (1 Corinthians 15:3-6, NIV).

HE IS THE ONLY WAY TO GOD "Jesus said to him, 'I am the way, and the truth, and the life; no one comes to the Father but through Me'" (John 14:6, NASB).

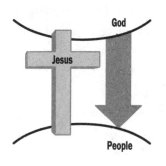

This diagram illustrates that God has bridged the gulf that separates us from Him by sending His Son, Jesus Christ, to die on the cross in our place to pay the penalty for our sins.

It is not enough just to know these three truths. . . .

4 — We Must Individually Receive Jesus Christ As Savior and Lord; Then We Can Know God Personally and Experience His Love

WE MUST RECEIVE CHRIST "As many as received Him, to them He gave the right to become children of God, even to those who believe in His name" (John 1:12, NASB).

WE RECEIVE CHRIST THROUGH FAITH "By grace you have been saved through faith; and that not of yourselves, it is the gift of God; not as a result of works, so that no one may boast" (Ephesians 2:8-9, NASB).

WHEN WE RECEIVE CHRIST, WE EXPERIENCE A NEW BIRTH (Read John 3:1-8.)

WE RECEIVE CHRIST BY PERSONAL INVITATION [Christ speaking] "Behold, I stand at the door and knock; if anyone hears My voice and opens the door, I will come in to him" (Revelation 3:20, NASB).

Receiving Christ involves turning to God from self (repentance) and trusting Christ to come into our lives to forgive us of our sins and to make us what He wants us to be. Just to agree intellectually that Jesus Christ is the Son of God and that He died on the cross for our sins is not enough. Nor is it enough to have an emotional experience. We receive Jesus Christ by faith, as an act of our will.

These two circles represent two kinds of lives:

Self-Directed Life

S – Self is on the throne
†– Christ is outside the life
● – Interests are directed by self, often resulting in discord and frustration

Christ-Directed Life

†– Christ is in the life and on the throne
S –Self is yielding to Christ
● – Interests are directed by God, resulting in harmony with God's plan

Which circle best represents your life?
Which circle would you like to have represent your life?

The following explains how you can receive Christ:

YOU CAN RECEIVE CHRIST RIGHT NOW BY FAITH THROUGH PRAYER
(Prayer is talking with God.)

God knows your heart and is not so concerned with your words
as He is with the attitude of your heart. The following is a
suggested prayer:

> *Lord Jesus, I want to know You personally. Thank You for dying
> on the cross for my sins. I open the door of my life and receive You
> as my Savior and Lord. Thank You for forgiving my sins and
> giving me eternal life. Take control of the throne of my life. Make
> me the kind of person You want me to be.*

Does this prayer express the desire of your heart?

If it does, I invite you to pray this prayer right now, and Christ
will come into your life, as He promised.

HOW TO KNOW THAT CHRIST IS IN YOUR LIFE Did you receive
Christ into your life? According to His promise in Revelation
3:20, where is Christ right now in relation to you? Christ said that
He would come into your life. Would He mislead you? On what
authority do you know that God has answered your prayer? (The
trustworthiness of God Himself and His Word.)

THE BIBLE PROMISES ETERNAL LIFE TO ALL WHO RECEIVE CHRIST
"The testimony is this, that God has given us eternal life, and this life is in His Son. He who has the Son has the life; he who does not have the Son of God does not have the life. These things I have written to you who believe in the name of the Son of God, so that you may know that you have eternal life" (1 John 5:11-13, NASB).

Thank God often that Christ is in your life and that He will never leave you (Hebrews 13:5). You can know on the basis of His promise that Christ lives in you and that you have eternal life from the very moment you invite Him in. He will not deceive you.

An important reminder . . .

FEELINGS CAN BE UNRELIABLE You might have expectations about how you should feel after placing your trust in Christ. While feelings are important, they are unreliable indicators of your sincerity or the trustworthiness of God's promise. Our feelings change easily, but God's Word and His character remain constant. This illustration shows the relationship among *fact* (God and His Word), *faith* (our trust in God and His Word), and our *feelings*.

Fact: The chair is strong enough to support you.

Faith: You believe this chair will support you, so you sit in it.

Feeling: You may or may not feel comfortable in this chair, but it continues to support you.

The promise of God's Word, the Bible—not our feelings—is our authority. The Christian lives by faith (trust) in the trustworthiness of God Himself and His Word.

NOW THAT YOU HAVE ENTERED INTO A PERSONAL RELATIONSHIP WITH CHRIST . . . The moment you received Christ by faith, as an act of your will, many things happened, including the following:

- Christ came into your life (Revelation 3:20; Colossians 1:27).
- Your sins were forgiven (Colossians 1:14).
- You became a child of God (John 1:12).
- You received eternal life (John 5:24).
- You began the great adventure for which God created you (John 10:10; 2 Corinthians 5:17; 1 Thessalonians 5:18).

Can you think of anything more wonderful that could happen to you than entering into a personal relationship with Jesus Christ? Would you like to thank God in prayer right now for what He has done for you? By thanking God, you demonstrate your faith.

To enjoy your new relationship with God . . .

SUGGESTIONS FOR CHRISTIAN GROWTH Spiritual growth results from trusting Jesus Christ. "The righteous man shall live by faith"

(Galatians 3:11, NASB). A life of faith will enable you to trust God increasingly with every detail of your life and to practice the following:

G *Go* to God in prayer daily (John 15:7).

R *Read* God's Word daily (Acts 17:11); begin with the Gospel of John.

O *Obey* God moment by moment (John 14:21).

W *Witness* for Christ by your life and words (Matthew 4:19; John 15:8).

T *Trust* God for every detail of your life (1 Peter 5:7).

H *Holy Spirit*—allow Him to control and empower your daily life and witness (Galatians 5:16-17; Acts 1:8; Ephesians 5:18).

FELLOWSHIP IN A GOOD CHURCH God's Word admonishes us not to forsake "the assembling of ourselves together" (Hebrews 10:25, NKJV). Several logs burn brightly together, but put one aside on the cold hearth, and the fire goes out. So it is with your relationship with other Christians. If you do not belong to a church, do not wait to be invited. Take the initiative; call the pastor of a nearby church where Christ is honored and His Word is preached. Start this week, and make plans to attend regularly.

Satisfied?

Satisfaction: (n.) fulfillment of one's needs, longings, or desires

What words would you use to describe your current experience as a Christian?

Growing	Frustrated
Disappointing	Fulfilled
Forgiven	Stuck
Struggling	Joyful
Defeated	Exciting
Up and down	Empty
Discouraged	Duty
Intimate	Mediocre
Painful	Dynamic
Guilty	Vital
So-so	Others?

Do you desire more? Jesus said, "If anyone is thirsty, let him come to me and drink. Whoever believes in me, as the Scripture has said, streams of living water will flow from within him" (John 7:37-38, NIV).

What did Jesus mean? John, the biblical author, went on to explain, "By this he meant the Spirit, whom those who believed in him were later to receive. Up to that time the Spirit had not been given, since Jesus had not yet been glorified" (John 7:39, NIV).

Jesus promised that God's Holy Spirit would satisfy the thirst, or deepest longings, of all who believe in Jesus Christ. However, many Christians do not understand the Holy Spirit or how to experience Him in their daily lives.

The following principles will help you understand and enjoy God's Spirit:

The Divine Gift

Divine: (adj.) given by God

God has given us His Spirit so that we can experience intimacy with Him and enjoy all He has for us.

The Holy Spirit is the source of our deepest satisfaction.

THE HOLY SPIRIT IS GOD'S PERMANENT PRESENCE WITH US.
Jesus said, "I will ask the Father, and he will give you another Counselor to be with you forever—the Spirit of truth" (John 14:16-17, NIV).

THE HOLY SPIRIT ENABLES US TO UNDERSTAND AND EXPERIENCE ALL GOD HAS GIVEN US.
"We have not received the spirit of the world but the Spirit who is from God, that we may understand what God has freely given us" (1 Corinthians 2:12, NIV).

The Holy Spirit enables us to experience many things:

- a genuine new spiritual life (John 3:1-8)
- the assurance of being a child of God (Romans 8:15-16)
- the infinite love of God (Romans 5:5; Ephesians 3:18-19)

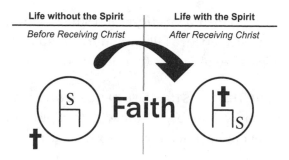

"The man without the Spirit does not accept the things that come from the Spirit of God, for they are foolishness to him, and he cannot understand them, because they are spiritually discerned" (1 Corinthians 2:14, NIV).

"The spiritual man makes judgments about all things. . . . We have the mind of Christ" (1 Corinthians 2:15-16, NIV).

"Those who are controlled by the Holy Spirit think about things that please the Spirit" (Romans 8:5, NLT).

Why are many Christians not satisfied in their experience with God?

The Present Danger

Danger: (n.) a thing that may cause injury, loss, or pain

We cannot experience intimacy with God and enjoy all He has for us if we fail to depend on His Spirit.

People who trust in their own efforts and strength to live the Christian life will experience failure and frustration, as will those who live to please themselves rather than God.

WE CANNOT LIVE THE CHRISTIAN LIFE IN OUR OWN STRENGTH.
"Are you so foolish? After beginning with the Spirit, are you now trying to attain your goal by human effort?" (Galatians 3:3, NIV).

WE CANNOT ENJOY ALL GOD DESIRES FOR US IF WE LIVE BY OUR SELF-CENTERED DESIRES.
"The sinful nature desires what is contrary to the Spirit, and the Spirit what is contrary to the sinful nature. They are in conflict with each other, so that you do not do what you want" (Galatians 5:17, NIV).

Three Kinds of Lifestyles

"Brothers, I could not address you as spiritual but as worldly—mere infants in Christ. I gave you milk, not solid food, for you were not yet ready for it. Indeed, you are still not ready. You are still worldly. For since there is jealousy and quarreling

Three Kinds of Lifestyles

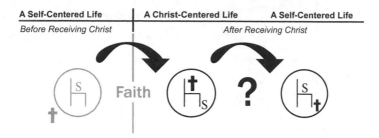

among you, are you not worldly? Are you not acting like mere men?" (1 Corinthians 3:1-3, NIV).

How can we develop a lifestyle of depending on the Spirit?

The Intimate Journey

Journey: (n.) any course from one experience to another

By walking in the Spirit we increasingly experience intimacy with God and enjoy all He has for us. Walking in the Spirit moment by moment is a lifestyle. It is learning to depend upon the Holy Spirit for His abundant resources as a way of life.

AS WE WALK IN THE SPIRIT, WE HAVE THE ABILITY TO LIVE A LIFE PLEASING TO GOD.
"So I say, live by the Spirit, and you will not gratify the desires of the sinful nature. . . . Since we live by the Spirit, let us keep in step with the Spirit" (Galatians 5:16, 25, NIV).

AS WE WALK IN THE SPIRIT, WE EXPERIENCE INTIMACY WITH GOD AND ALL HE HAS FOR US.
"The fruit of the Spirit is love, joy, peace, patience, kindness, goodness, faithfulness, gentleness and self-control" (Galatians 5:22-23, NIV).

Faith (trust in God and His promises) is the only way a Christian can live by the Spirit.

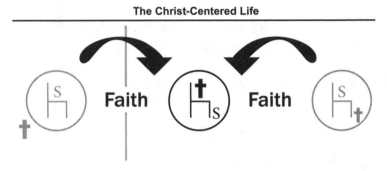

The Christ-Centered Life

SPIRITUAL BREATHING is a powerful word picture that can help you experience moment-by-moment dependence upon the Spirit.

Exhale: Confess your sin the moment you become aware of it—agree with God concerning it and thank Him for His forgiveness, according to 1 John 1:9 and Hebrews 10:1-25. Confession requires repentance—a change in attitude and action.

Inhale: Surrender control of your life to Christ, and rely upon the Holy Spirit to fill you with His presence and power by faith, according to His command (Ephesians 5:18) and promise (1 John 5:14-15).

How does the Holy Spirit fill us with His power?

The Empowering Presence

Empower: (v.) to give ability to

We are filled with the Spirit by faith, enabling us to experience intimacy with God and enjoy all He has for us.

The essence of the Christian life is what God does in and through us, not what we do for God. Christ's life is reproduced in the believer by the power of the Holy Spirit. To be filled with the Spirit is to be directed and empowered by Him.

BY FAITH, WE EXPERIENCE GOD'S POWER THROUGH THE HOLY SPIRIT. "I pray that out of his glorious riches he may strengthen you with power through his Spirit in your inner being, so that Christ may dwell in your hearts through faith" (Ephesians 3:16-17, NIV).

THREE IMPORTANT QUESTIONS TO ASK YOURSELF:

1. Am I ready now to surrender control of my life to our Lord Jesus Christ? (Romans 12:1-2).
2. Am I ready now to confess my sins? (1 John 1:9). Sin grieves God's Spirit (Ephesians 4:30). But God in His love has forgiven all of your sins—past, present, and future—because Christ has died for you.
3. Do I sincerely desire to be directed and empowered by the Holy Spirit? (John 7:37-39).

BY FAITH, CLAIM THE FULLNESS OF THE SPIRIT ACCORDING TO HIS COMMAND AND PROMISE:

God *commands* us to be filled with the Spirit.

"Be filled with the Spirit" (Ephesians 5:18, NIV).

God *promises* He will always answer when we pray according to His will.

"This is the confidence we have in approaching God: that if we ask anything according to his will, he hears us. And if we know that he hears us—whatever we ask—we know that we have what we asked of him" (1 John 5:14-15, NIV).

How to pray to be filled with the Holy Spirit . . .

The Turning Point

Turning point: (n.) time when a decisive change occurs

We are filled with the Holy Spirit by faith alone.

Sincere prayer is one way of expressing our faith. The following is a suggested prayer:

> *Dear Father, I need You. I acknowledge that I have sinned against You by directing my own life. I thank You that You have forgiven my sins through Christ's death on the cross for me. I now invite Christ to again take His place on the throne of my life. Fill me with the Holy Spirit as You commanded me to be filled and as You promised in Your Word that You would do if I asked in faith.*

*I pray this in the name of Jesus. I now thank You for filling me
with the Holy Spirit and directing my life.*

Does this prayer express the desire of your heart? If so, you can
pray right now and trust God to fill you with His Holy Spirit.

HOW TO KNOW THAT YOU ARE FILLED BY THE HOLY SPIRIT:

- Did you ask God to fill you with the Holy Spirit?
- Do you know that you are now filled with the Holy Spirit?
- On what authority? (On the trustworthiness of God
  Himself and His Word: Hebrews 11:6; Romans 14:22-23)

As you continue to depend on God's Spirit moment by moment,
you will experience and enjoy intimacy with God and all He has
for you—a truly rich and satisfying life.

An important reminder . . .

DO NOT DEPEND ON FEELINGS

The promise of God's Word, the Bible—not our feelings—is our
authority. The Christian lives by faith (trust) in the trustworthiness of God Himself and His Word. Flying in an airplane can
illustrate the relationship among fact (God and His Word), faith
(our trust in God and His Word), and feeling (the result of our
faith and obedience) (John 14:21).

To be transported by an airplane, we must place our faith in
the trustworthiness of the aircraft and the pilot who flies it. Our
feelings of confidence or fear do not affect the ability of the

airplane to transport us, though they do affect how much we enjoy the trip. In the same way, we as Christians do not depend on feelings or emotions, but we place our faith (trust) in the trustworthiness of God and the promises of His Word.

Now That You Are Filled with the Holy Spirit

Thank God that the Spirit will enable you:

- to glorify Christ with your life (John 16:14)
- to grow in your understanding of God and His Word (1 Corinthians 2:14-15)
- to live a life pleasing to God (Galatians 5:16-23)

REMEMBER THE PROMISE OF JESUS:

"But you will receive power when the Holy Spirit comes on you; and you will be my witnesses in Jerusalem, and in all Judea and Samaria, and to the ends of the earth" (Acts 1:8, NIV).

If you would like additional resources on the Holy Spirit, please go to **www.nlpdirect.com**.

Adapted from *Have You Made the Wonderful Discovery of the Spirit-Filled Life?* Written by Bill Bright, © 1966. Published by New*Life* Publications, P.O. Box 593684, Orlando, FL 32859.

Notes

Chapter 3: Unmerited Favor
1. Donald Grey Barnhouse, *Let Me Illustrate: Stories, Anecdotes, Illustrations* (Westwood, N.J.: Revell, 1967), 355.

Chapter 4: A Glorious Gift
1. Charles R. Swindoll, *Growing Strong in the Seasons of Life* (Portland, Ore.: Multnomah, 1983), 66.
2. Ibid., 67.
3. Ibid.

Chapter 5: A Surrendered Lifestyle
1. Steve Lawson, *Absolutely Sure: Settle the Question of Eternal Life* (Sisters, Ore.: Multnomah, 1999), 101.

Chapter 6: Giving Up on Guilt
1. Watchman Nee, *The Normal Christian Life* (London: Kingsway Publications, 1961), 76.
2. Max Lucado, *In the Grip of Grace* (Dallas, Tex.: Word, 1996), 122–23.

Chapter 9: Being Aware of the Spirit
1. Vernon C. Grounds, *Radical Commitment: Getting Serious about Christian Growth* (Portland, Ore.: Multnomah, 1984), 38.

Chapter 10: What's a Woman to Do?
1. Phyllis Thompson, *A Transparent Woman: The Compelling Story of Gladys Aylward* (Grand Rapids, Mich.: Zondervan, 1971), 20. As quoted in Ruth Tucker, *From Jerusalem to Irian Jaya: A Biographical History of Christian Missions* (Grand Rapids, Mich.: Zondervan, 1983), 254.

Chapter 13: Conversations That Count
1. Joni Eareckson Tada, *Secret Strength: For Those Who Search* (Portland, Ore.: Multnomah Press, 1988), 307.
2. Ibid., 309.

Chapter 16: Growing Up Gracefully
1. Quoted in Gordon S. Jackson, *Quotes for the Journey* (Colorado Springs, Colo.: NavPress, 2000), 87.

Resources

My Heart in His Hands: *Spring: Renew a Steadfast Spirit within Me.* Spring—renewal is everywhere; we are reminded to cry out to God, "Renew a steadfast spirit within me." The first of four books in Vonette Bright's devotional series, this book will give fresh spiritual vision and hope to women of all ages. ISBN 1-56399-161-6

My Heart in His Hands: *Summer: Set Me Free Indeed.* Summer—a time of freedom. Are there bonds that keep you from God's best? With this devotional, a few moments daily can help you draw closer to the One who gives true freedom. This is the second of four in the devotional series. ISBN 1-56399-162-4

My Heart in His Hands: *Autumn: I Delight Greatly in His Hands.* Do you stop to appreciate the blessings God has given you? Spend time delighting in God with book three in this devotional series. ISBN 1-56399-163-2

My Heart in His Hands: *Winter: Lead Me in the Way Everlasting.* We all need guidance, and God is the ultimate leader. These daily moments with God will help you to rely on His leadership. The final in the four-book devotional series. ISBN 1-56399-164-0

My Heart in His Hands: Bible Study Guides. Designed to complement the four devotional books in this series, the Bible Study Guides allow a woman to examine God's Word and gain perspective on the issues that touch her life. Each study highlights a biblical character and includes an inspirational portrait of a woman who served God.

A Renewed Heart (1-56399-176-4)
A Nurturing Heart (1-56399-177-2)
A Woman's Heart (1-56399-178-0)
A Free Heart (1-56399-179-9)
A Wise Heart (1-56399-180-2)
A Caring Heart (1-56399-181-0)

The Joy of Hospitality: Fun Ideas for Evangelistic Entertaining. Cowritten with Barbara Ball, this practical book tells how to share your faith through hosting barbecues, coffees, holiday parties, and other events in your home. ISBN 1-56399-057-1

The Joy of Hospitality Cookbook. Filled with uplifting scriptures and quotations, this cookbook contains hundreds of delicious recipes, hospitality tips, sample menus, and family traditions that are sure to make your entertaining a memorable and eternal success. Cowritten with Barbara Ball. ISBN 1-56399-077-6

The Greatest Lesson I've Ever Learned: For Women. In this treasury of inspiring, real-life experiences, twenty-three prominent women of faith share their "greatest lessons." Does God have faith- and character-building lessons for you in their rich, heartwarming stories? ISBN 1-56399-085-7

Beginning Your Journey of Joy. This adaptation of the *Four Spiritual Laws* speaks in the language of today's women and offers a slightly feminine approach to sharing God's love with your neighbors, friends, and family members. ISBN 1-56399-093-8

About the Author

$\mathcal{V}$onette Bright, along with her late husband, Dr. William R. Bright, cofounded Campus Crusade for Christ. She earned a Bachelor of Science degree in home economics from Texas Woman's University and did graduate work in the field of education at the University of Southern California. Vonette taught in Los Angeles schools before joining Bill full-time in Campus Crusade. Vonette has two married sons and four grandchildren.

Vonette's commitment to helping reach the world for Christ has fueled a passion for prayer and a desire to help others develop a heart for God. She serves as chair for The Bright Media Foundation and maintains an amazing schedule from her home in Orlando, Florida.

The Woman Within, the first in a series of four nonfiction books designed to complement the four novels cowritten with Nancy Moser, has one goal: to see women of faith connecting, loving, caring, serving, and supporting each other with such genuine love that women who do not know Christ will be drawn to those who do and will want to meet Him.